YEHR-KUUND

TROPHY WHITETAILS

THE SECRETS TO PUTTING ALL OF THE ODDS IN YOUR FAVOR

by Joe Brooks

Photography by Joe Brooks and Mark Lodzinski

Year-Round Trophy Whitetails
The Secrets To Putting All Of The Odds In Your Favor
by Joe Brooks

© 2006 by Joe Brooks

All rights reserved. No part of this book may be reproduced or transmitted in any form or by any means, electronic or mechanical, including photocopying, recording or by any information storage and retrieval system, without written permission from the author, except for brief quotations in a review.

Published by:
Cabin Fever Publications
Post Office Box 366
Sylvania, Ohio 43560

Library of Congress Catalog Number: 2006905152
ISBN: 0-9785903-6-8

This book is dedicated to the most wonderful woman in the world. My beautiful wife, Pat, has put up with my whitetail hunting antics for a very long time. Her understanding and love means everything.

Acknowledgements

My journey hunting whitetails has been a good one. I have spent as much time and thought into pursuing this magnificent animal as anyone I know. There are very few moments during the day or night that I am not fretting over how I can outsmart this creature of great deception and will for survival.

Even though I am fortunate with all of my hard-earned success, it has not all come to me of my own accord and persistence. Therefore, I must thank a few outstanding human beings, close friends and loved ones.

To my wife, Pat, who has stood by my side through everything. She understands my drive and supports me even though she is a whole-hearted animal lover. She patiently waits for me to come home from the woods and takes care of me the way no one else ever could. I am forever grateful that she is there for me, and I owe her everything.

To Gerald Gerity who first took me up north to chase those spooky does with our recurves. He is a big part of the fire that burns in me to chase whitetails.

To Dr. Mark Wentz who put me back together again after the accident.

To Paul Brunner who I have never met but read his book so long ago called, "Tree Stand Hunting." This one book changed how I thought about deer hunting and pushed me in the right direction. I could only hope to meet him some day.

To Gene Wensel and his brother, Barry, whose antics on camera and in written form showed me how to enjoy life and the outdoors in a way I never knew existed.

To all of those wonderful people, farmers and landowners who were kind enough to allow me to hunt on their land. Especially Carlton Reeves who is a great friend and as fine a person you would ever want to meet.

Special thanks go to all of the good, responsible and ethical hunters I have met over the years. Even though there are too many names to mention, they have all showed true sportsmanship in the field.

To Beth Lodzinski who tolerates everything I put her husband through.

Finally, to Mark Lodzinski, the finest hunting partner anyone could ever have. His drive to outsmart trophy whitetails is tremendous, and it is what keeps me going even during the bleakest hours of the season. No one has helped me better than he to sort out the information that we constantly absorb while hunting trophy whitetails. I never have to look back for him as he is ahead of me in every task. Everyone should be as lucky as I am to hunt with such a great person. He is my best friend, and I owe him tremendously.

Last, but not least, I cannot forget to give thanks to the magnificent whitetail deer themselves. They are what makes my heart beat and my blood flow . . . for that I am forever grateful.

Contents

Chapter

1	Where Are Those Trophy Bucks?	11
2	Post Season	29
3	Spring	45
4	Summer	65
5	Pre-season	79
6	Low Profile Hunting	93
7	Clothing and Equipment	113
8	Weapons of Choice	129
9	Scents, Calling, Decoys and Baiting	139
10	The Early Season	149
11	November	157
12	Late Season	175
13	Odds-n-Ends	181
14	Three Seasons	187

A fantastic end to one of my hunting seasons.

Introduction

You are about to go on an incredible journey. The trophy whitetail buck is the most sought after big game animal in North America. Thirty years of fascination about this animal has brought me to this point in my life where I want to share with you all the information in this book.

My hunting partner, Mark Lodzinski, and I have approximately sixty years of whitetail hunting between us, and have spent thousands of hours watching these magnificent animals from our tree stands. We have tried every hunting tactic and gimmick in print trying to bring those monster bucks within range of our weapons.

Many of these tactics that seemed to work great on non pressured whitetails in some of the more unpopulated states, worked with rather poor success in our more populated and pressured hunting areas. The few times that they did work were in areas where the animals did not receive the same tremendous hunting pressure as the rest of the state.

Hunters are always looking for a quick shortcut to success, and this keeps such gimmicks and strategies alive. Giant advertising campaigns, doctored hunting videos and the lust for money by the manufacturers lead you to believe, if you use their product, you will gain instant results. The truth is that their products do have limited results, but most of the time your odds are low that they will work.

Many tactics touted by some of the better known hunters are regional, and the deer in those areas are susceptible to them. Most hunters become disappointed when these tactics do not work in their area, and are disillusioned by what they have read, bought or learned.

This book is about to change your hunting success forever. The information in this book is not regional in nature, and is the only system that will work anywhere trophy whitetail bucks are found, and is not a gimmick. Every bit of information in this book will up your odds, whether you just want to hunt deer or you want to take home that trophy of a lifetime.

In the past ten years or so, Mark and I have placed over thirty mature whitetail bucks on our walls. Every single one of them were taken using the tactics you are about to learn. There are going to be many well-known trophy hunters out there upset due to the release of this information and many other known hunters may learn something.

The most important thing is that there has been nothing left out of this book. There are no missing pieces that no one will tell you about. This book is going to "drop the bomb" or "let the cat out of the bag" so to speak. Everything in this book is just as we do it ourselves.

Do not worry about destroying this book as you read it many times over. It would make me proud if you took a marker and highlighted all of the information on these pages. You will find a lot of information that has never been in print before. So read on and get prepared for the best deer hunting years of your life!!

Chapter 1

Where Are Those Trophy Bucks?

You are probably reading this book right now wondering if you have just wasted your hard earned money. Is this book really going to help you find and give you a chance to take home a trophy whitetail of a lifetime? You may even think that there are no big bucks living in the area that you hunt. There is only one thing you must learn before you use any of the information in this book. Before you can plan on hunting trophy whitetails you must first know where they live.

Every state that contains a deer herd has places that larger-than-average bucks grow. You may think that there are no big deer close to your home, but if you look at any state record book, you will see that every county in your state has had deer taken that would make any trophy hunter proud. In this chapter you will learn that even though most of the hunting population lives in states with a poorly managed deer herd that is heavily hunted, you still have trophy whitetails within your reach.

What Is a Trophy?

First we must decide on what makes up a trophy animal. To many people it could be their first deer. To others it may be their first buck. Many may be happy with anything that has six points or more on its rack. In this book we are only going to talk about adult animals, as these are the bucks that most people dream about at night. In most states, any animal that makes it past their third

**This buck is a trophy,
even though he just has two large spikes.**

birthday should be considered a trophy. Hunters should never decide on whether a buck is a trophy just on score alone. Many old, gnarly bucks with a lot of bone on their heads score pretty poorly. In highly pressured areas, like most of us live in, a three and a half year old buck is as hard to kill as a five or six and a half year old animal in states like Kansas, Iowa and Illinois. Most fairly successful trophy hunters from these states would do poorly hunting areas that most of us are restricted to hunting.

Food, Water and Cover

For deer to survive they must have three essential things. They must have enough food, water and cover to make it through the year. Realize that deer will relocate as many times as needed to meet these needs through the year. In the following chapters you will learn how to key in on which one of these items a deer has the least of, and how to use this to your advantage. After these three things there is only one more need to be met for an animal to grow to trophy size and age.

For any buck to live long enough to grow a large set of antlers, he must live in a place where no hunter has a chance to kill him most of the time or where no hunter has ever thought of hunting. As you read about some of the following places mentioned in this chapter, you might realize that many of these places are close to your home. While keeping this in mind, the light bulb might pop on and open a whole new door to your trophy hunting possibilities.

State Laws

State laws are one of the main determinations on whether your state holds more trophy whitetails than another. Don't fret because every state with a population of whitetails has some trophy bucks, but the laws in your state may swing more of the odds in your favor.

States with gun seasons that do not coincide with the rut usually have a healthier trophy buck population. For

**This is what can happen
with the right food, water and cover.**

example, Michigan's gun season starts on November 15th, which is usually during the rut. Ohio does not start its gun season until the end of November or the beginning of December when most of the breeding is over. This one reason alone helps Ohio claim more trophy deer than Michigan.

States where you are only allowed one buck per season usually have a healthier trophy buck population. Michigan allows two bucks per season. On the other hand Ohio only allows one buck per season. Indiana recently went from two bucks to one buck per season. Indiana's trophy potential has increased greatly due to this change. States like Pennsylvania now have areas with antler restrictions that have changed their trophy population for the better in just a couple of years.

There are three times during the season when the odds are best to get close to a big buck during the daylight hours. The one most talked about and written about is the period called the rut. This may be the greatest time of year to connect on a monster whitetail, but there are a couple of other times when the odds may be in your favor.

If you live in a state where you have hunting seasons as early as September when the bucks are still in bachelor groups, it will put a few more of the odds in your favor. This is a great time to get a chance at a trophy of a lifetime, as the bucks are easy to pattern and are not as wired as they will be later in the season.

On the other hand, if your regulations allow hunting in late December or January, you will be able to hunt during another one of the best times of the year to take a trophy buck home. Whitetails will group together on high-energy food sources, and many times you will see trophy bucks out feeding in the middle of the day.

Evolution of a State

First, let's look at how a state changes through the years and how this affects the trophy hunting possibilities. Most trophy deer hunting states start out with a relatively low human population and have a growing deer herd. Many of

Small protected properties can grow bucks like this.

our Western and Plain states such as Iowa and Kansas are like this today.

Most states at this early stage consist of large farms containing hundreds or even thousands of acres. Usually there are only a couple of people that hunt these farms. They will have quality hunting for large bucks, but will not harvest or put very much pressure on very many animals. This allows for a healthy deer herd with a good age structure containing many older bucks. This is why many people travel to such states today, and why most of the deer hunting TV shows are filmed in such places.

As the human population grows, as does the need for land, many farms shrink to a few hundred acres or less. What this means is that if you still have two hunters per farm the pressure on the deer herd has grown tremendously. For example if you only had two hunters on a 1,200 acre farm in the past, and now this farm has been split into twelve 100 acre farms allowing two hunters on them, you now have twenty four hunters trying to kill a big buck on the same amount of property as the original two.

In most states in the Midwest and the East, the farms have shrunk to 20 or 40 acres. Many of these farms have four or more hunters on them. Do you realize how many hunters are on our 1,200 acres now? One would wonder how any trophy bucks survive. Please don't give up though, because there is light at the end of the tunnel.

Finally, as the human population grows, many people move out to the country on small 5 and 10 acre lots. These people love to watch wildlife and most do not allow hunting. This gives the deer a sanctuary to grow old in. Furthermore, cities get bigger, as do townships, which still hold cover for the deer to survive in. Many new sanctuaries are created during this time that will hold monster bucks big enough to make any trophy hunter happy. Just remember one thing. If you cannot hunt in a sanctuary, you may be able to hunt next to one.

**By working hard
I was able to take this buck out of a sanctuary.**

Break Lines

Most books that you read will talk about break lines being a change in types of cover from one to another. This is often stated as the field meeting the woods, pines meeting the hardwoods, or thick bedding cover meeting the open timber. Even though these definitions are correct and are very useful, in the new world where the trophy hunter hunts bucks in highly pressured areas, there is a new definition of break lines.

A break line is any boundary where a section of land that does not allow deer hunting and contains a deer herd borders land that it is possible, and legal, to get permission to hunt. Go back and read that line once again as it is one of the most important concepts for today's trophy hunter in pressured areas. Under these conditions only one acre could become a honey hole for trophy whitetails. The following examples are places where most of the trophy whitetails in a highly pressured state live. Finding a place to hunt next to them, or if you are really lucky and it is legal, obtaining the right to hunt in them, will bring you close to the largest whitetail bucks anyone anywhere has a chance to hunt. Later in this book you will learn when and/or how to get these bucks to leave the protection of these sanctuaries. If you are lucky enough to hunt in one of these places you will learn how to keep a low profile so that these animals do not know they are being hunted.

City limits are usually our closest and most often overlooked break lines to check out. Many monster bucks die of old age within large metropolitan cities. In many of these cities the deer herds have exploded to giant proportions. Some cities now have restricted hunting rules within the city limits. If not, there usually are many places bordering these city limits where you can find a large adult buck to hunt.

Townships are often overlooked as many people think that they do not allow hunting. Many do, especially for bow hunters. Those that do not are growing your next big buck for you, if you can find a place to hunt next to the line.

Large country subdivisions, Boy Scout camps, Girl Scout camps, church camps, golf courses, put and take

This buck was taken within fifty yards of the state line.

pheasant operations, airports, city metro parks, state parks, and federal wildlife areas hold tons of mature whitetails. How many places like this can you think of? You should be able to find many of these areas close to home. If you follow the steps in the next chapters, you may even get a chance to hunt within the boundaries of some of these areas. Many also have controlled hunts, which you can apply for.

Most people overlook private property that does not allow hunting. Many acres that are owned by private individuals or corporations hold the bucks you are looking for if they do not allow hunting. Power plants are a good example of this.

Many deer hunting TV personalities and deer hunting authors hunt these types of places so that they can fill their walls with trophy bucks. They just do not want you to think that they hunt next to sanctuaries like the ones you are learning about. This is why this book was written so that you can have a chance to kill giant whitetails just like the big names of the sport.

Finally there is one break line that I have never seen in print. This is the concept of hunting along state lines that have different hunting seasons. For example Michigan has its gun season starting every year on the 15th through the 30th of November; Whereas Ohio starts its deer gun hunting season the first Monday after Thanksgiving until the following Saturday. In both of these states you can only hunt with shotguns along the state lines. In many years the Michigan season is done before the Ohio season starts. On the opening day of Michigan gun season, the deer run across the state line into Ohio. Then, after the Michigan gun season closes and the Ohio gun season opens, the deer run back across the state line into Michigan. These deer rarely see a gun hunter and have a great chance to grow into old mature bucks. Wow! I bet you are thinking hard on that one. Just think of your own neighboring states and how their rules apply.

This buck lived in a scout camp.

State Land and Timber Companies

State land is normally not the place you should look for trophy bucks in a highly pressured area. Giant whitetails do exist on state land but your odds of killing one are slim. For some this may be your only option until you find a better alternative. Don't give up because there are a couple of options that may work in your favor though.

If your state has large tracts of state land open to hunting, you may be able to get far enough from the road to be able to hunt deer that are not as pressured. Some areas have rivers that you can navigate to get further back in or islands that very few venture out on. During the rut you may be able to catch a large, mature buck traveling during any time of the day looking for does. Gun season may also force movement of some animals that normally would not venture out of their thick bedding areas during daylight hours.

Large swamps or giant impenetrable thickets may likewise hold the deer of your dreams if you can get into them or get the animals to come out of them.

Timber and paper companies also are an alternative that many hunters never think about. Most allow deer hunting in one form or another. The clear cuts left behind can also become the best big buck sanctuary in the area. You will learn how to find these companies in the upcoming chapter.

What the Record Books Show

One easy way to find out where the big bucks are coming from in your state is to check the record books. You can check the Boone and Crockett, Pope and Young, and your state's record books. These are a good source, but do not rely on them too heavily, as they are just a good indicator on what counties have what it takes to grow trophy whitetails.

Local deer shows may even be a better bet to find out where the big bucks hide, as they usually display last year's heads for all to see. Many may be mature whitetails that did not score well enough to make it in the record books or

The record books can help show you where to hunt.

their owners did not want to put their trophy in the book. Take a pen and paper and write down the counties where these bucks came from. If you do this you quickly will find a pattern. This is the most recent information you can find about where the big bucks in your state are coming from.

Last but not least, you may check with a couple of your local taxidermists, as they are a wealth of knowledge, if you can pry it out of them.

Full Time Job

Hunting just trophy whitetails is a year-round, full-time job if you really want to succeed properly. It is hard to do if you have many other hobbies. You will have to decide whether you want to be good at a few different sports or great at one particular sport. Following are a couple of ideas to think about before you continue to the next chapter.

Finding a place to hunt where the hunting pressure is low greatly improves your odds of finding a trophy whitetail versus hunting in a highly pressured area. Recognize though, even the most pressured areas have some spots rarely hunted.

The closer you hunt to home, the better use of time you have to chase that trophy. Use your vacation to travel to your farther hunting areas. Then spend the rest of your time near home and you can find more time to hunt between working hours, and you can go hunting during the peak times more often.

If you do find evidence of one big buck in your area, this is a great thing, but, keep in mind it is better to hunt an area with a few big bucks versus putting all your eggs in one basket and hunting just one animal. Ask yourself one question. Would you rather try and hunt one trophy buck that lives within a five square mile area or would you rather hunt five trophy bucks that all live within a one square mile area? Do not forget that it is all about the odds.

Finally, bear in mind that it is better to have ten perfect stands on ten different properties than to have ten mediocre stands on one property. You may have to read that last line a couple of times to fully understand it and remember it, as

Mark scored on this great whitetail by working year-round.

it is one of the most important things to know when hunting mature bucks in highly pressured areas.

Remember, odds, odds, odds, and odds!!!!

This is what happens
when you put all of the odds in your favor.

Chapter 2

Post Season

This chapter is probably the most important chapter of all in your strategy to hunt trophy whitetails. Post season is considered the time immediately after your deer season closes. This could be January, February or March depending on the hunting regulations in your state. If you start working towards each season at this time of year instead of waiting until October, you will have the best odds ever of harvesting the biggest buck of your life. This is absolutely the best time to scout your existing properties looking for funnels, bedding cover, sheds, etc.

At this time of year the woods will look just like it will during the fall after leaf drop. You furthermore do not have to worry about spooking animals at this time of year. You can check out your existing properties when the woods will be an exact copy of the way it will look during the rut next fall.

It is very important to check out the cover density of your hunting spots at this time. Usually in the fall you set your stands in what you may think is a thick cover funnel. Then after leaf drop you find yourself out of place and in the open. The cover at your stand site now is too thin for a mature buck to feel secure traveling during daylight hours. You then have to decide whether to sit there and suffer or move your stand. If you do move your stand it can create a lot of disturbance, which might destroy your set up. Making more than a couple of mistakes like this will drastically lower your odds during the hunting season. If you pick out your stand sites during the post season, you will know exactly what it will look like in the late fall. Then hopefully you will not have to adjust your stands.

This is also the time when you should start looking for new places to hunt mature bucks. How do you accomplish this you ask? In this chapter you will learn step-by-step just how to do this from your desk at home.

Atlas & Gazetteer

First you need to get yourself a State Atlas & Gazetteer from Delorme. These maps of each state will show you topography, roads, and timber, streams, camps, and state and city parks, all drawn from aerial photography. These maps are very precise. All of your other information and other maps should be compared to them.

When you open one of these map books to the page where you live, or the area you think you might like to hunt, you should immediately see many examples of the kind of sanctuaries you learned about in chapter one. Mark these on your map. These are the places to start your search for that trophy whitetail.

You can find DeLorme Atlas & Gazetteers at almost any bookstore or most major sporting goods stores. Or you can contact them directly at:

> ➤ DeLorme, P.O. Box 298 Yarmouth, Maine 04096, Phone # (207) 846–7000

Or you may contact them online at:

> ➤ http://www.delorme.com

Graphic Street Guide

A graphic street guide of your city is likewise very useful. These maps should show you exactly where the city property lines are located. You will be amazed that these property lines may not be where you think. This can open

Post Season 31

**DeLorme maps are a great place
to start your search for trophy bucks.**

up many possibilities for places to hunt. You should be able to find them at any bookstore, carryout or grocery store.

Plat Books

Once you decide which county or counties you wish to search for new big buck hot spots in, you need to purchase a plat book of that county. Plat books will show you all land ownership, larger than usually five acres, in that county. These books are divided by township and then section, which usually consists of one square mile. You can buy these books from a couple of sources:

- County Treasury Office

- County Soil and Water Conservation Office

- Farm Bureau

- Rockford Map Publishers

Rockford Map Publishers seem to sell some of the best plat books of all. You can contact them at:

- Rockford Map Publishers Inc., P.O. Box 6126 Rockford, Illinois 61125, Phone # (800) 446-3530

Or you may contact them online at:

- http://www.rockfordmap.com

If they do not sell the plat book of the county you want to hunt, the next best place to find a plat book is your County Treasury Office.

When you receive your plat book, highlight any area that a buck may find a sanctuary in which to grow into trophy proportions. As you learned earlier, areas to look for are city limits, city parks, state parks, federal wildlife refuges, scout camps, church camps, golf courses, large

Post Season 33

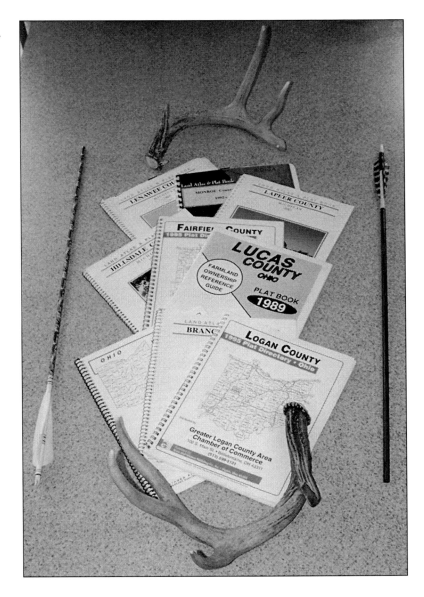

Plat books are the key to property owners.

swamps and large farms just to name a few. These are the places to begin your search to ask for permission to hunt on or next to. By checking them against your Delorme map you will get an idea what kind of cover grows there.

Aerial Photographs

This is how you scout from the comfort of your home. Anyone who says that they know every inch of the property they hunt, and have never seen it from the air, is usually quite surprised when they see an aerial photo of their property. Almost every stand you set will be decided on by these photos, long before you ever step foot on the property. Here are a few sources to get these photos:

- http://www.terraserverusa.com
- http://www.mapcard.com
- County Mapping Department

Once you have decided where you want to concentrate your efforts you should go to the Internet and get on Terra Server. This website will allow you to get free aerial photos of your area. Compare these with your plat books and you will start to see where you need to gain permission.

When you finally decide where you want to concentrate your efforts, go to your County Mapping Department. This is usually located near the County Treasury Office. Here you will be able to purchase two-foot square aerial photos of your properties. Sometimes the local Farm Bureau might as well carry these photos. These pictures are taken in conjunction with the townships and sections in your plat books. Please ask for property line overlays on these photos.

These photos are usually taken during the winter and will give you a good idea of what the cover looks like. You can usually tell the difference between types of cover like bedding thickets, pines, and hardwoods. You can also see all ponds and lakes. Houses and buildings likewise show

Aerial photos are key to understanding deer movement.

up. You may even be surprised at the fact that some strips of cover do not go the exact direction that you thought. This really helps in stand placement. These are the most useful photos to be found and sometimes you can even locate deer trails on them.

County Phone Books

In the next chapter you will learn how to approach landowners to gain permission to hunt. Many of these landowners do not live on the property you are interested in. The county phone book may show you where they live. If they are not listed, you can go to the County Treasury Office and they can tell you where the property taxes are being sent. Although this is public record, please treat the people at the Treasury Office with respect, as they are our important link to giant whitetails.

County Auditors Website

If you go to the Internet and do a search for your county Auditors' website you may get a surprise. Many of the Auditors' offices today are putting a link on their website where you can look at all of the properties in that county on aerial photos. They provide right on the web all of the information you are looking for. Information such as property lines, owner's names, addresses of the property, and addresses where the owner lives. This is good to know, if they do not live on the property. This information is much more up to date than plat books, as they only print plat books about every three years. These websites are often updated weekly. If your county offers this service, you are lucky.

Post Season 37

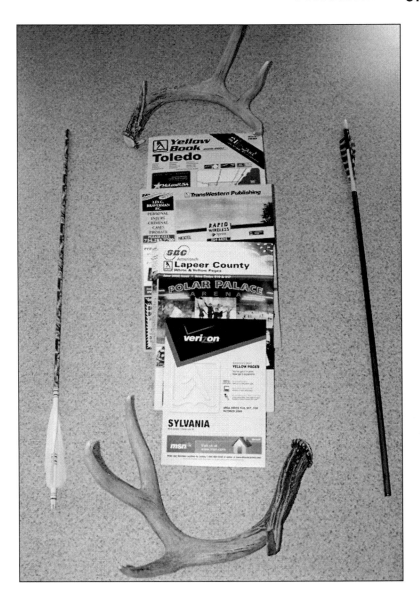

**County phone books
are great for finding landowners.**

National White Pages Phone Directories

Some property owners may live out of state. You may want to make an introductory phone call to them, followed up with a letter asking permission to hunt for deer. You can call Information, if you know the city they live in, or there are a few websites that you can try. Here are a couple of good ones:

> http://www.whitepages.com

> http://www.directory.superpages.com/people.jsp

Road Atlas

You may be surprised but a common road atlas or a folding state map may show you where some big whitetails are in your state.

Take a protractor and draw a sixty-mile circle around each big city in your state. Then draw a thirty-mile circle around all of the medium size towns. Most people from big cities do not like to travel more than sixty miles from home to hunt. Most people from small cities rarely travel more than thirty miles to chase deer.

Now look at any area outside of these circles. Whitetails in these areas usually receive less hunting pressure than most. These areas are prime spots for you to start your search for that trophy buck.

You probably never thought there were so many ways to find property and landowners!

Public Hunting on Private Lands

Many states offer certain programs which allow hunters to hunt private land. Landowners sign up for these programs and usually receive a small fee from the state. These lands are not usually the best place to start your search. They may be a better choice than public land though, as not as many hunters know of these programs.

You can learn about them if you contact your state's Department of Natural Resources.

There is one tip you can use on these lands. Most hunters have to enter the property from one direction. Go to the opposite side of the property and ask the neighbor if you can cross his property to hunt. As long as you do not hunt his property most will allow you to cross. Early in the morning many animals may move by your stand because the other hunters are coming in from the other side. You may also be able to gain access to a part of the property that the other hunters cannot get to. This may create a small sanctuary to hunt all by yourself.

**Your post season work
is the most important to your success.**

Topographic Maps

Topographic maps have been included last. This is due to the fact that unless you are hunting large expanses of cover that are rather hilly, you will probably have no need for them. Plus, the Delorme Atlas will show topography.

There have been many articles and at least one good book written on how to use them. There will be a list of helpful books in a later chapter. If you do find that you need a good topographic map, here is where to get them. Some sporting goods stores, Farm Bureau Offices, National Forest Offices, and County Soil and Water Conservation Offices may carry them.

For the best way to get them, contact:

> USGS Information Services, P.O. Box 25286, Denver, CO 80225, Phone # (888) 275 – 8747

Or you may contact them online at:

> http://www.usgs.gov

Your phone and computer are two of the best scouting tools that you own. If you learn to use them properly, you will cut your scouting time in half. Big whitetails are not found behind every bush. By using these tools, you will find bigger whitetails than you have ever seen before. You will additionally locate numbers of quality animals.

Shed Hunting

February is the time we should be looking for quality animals that we might have a chance at next fall. Shed hunting is one of the ways we can locate animals that survived the past hunting season. Combining shed hunting with a little scouting can be a great way to learn your property better, and give you a way to enjoy the outdoors during the off season.

As you learned earlier, one nice thing about this time of year is that the woods look just as they will in the late fall. Whitetails can lose their antlers any time between late December and late March. Don't give up after just one trip to the woods. Besides, any time you look where multiple mature bucks live, your odds go up greatly that you may find sheds. Do not get disappointed if you do not find any sheds. This does not mean that there are no mature bucks on your property.

Due to the smaller farms in the eastern United States, many deer cross more than one or two property lines during a twenty-four hour period. Your mature bucks may drop their antlers on property you do not have access to. As well some animals may relocate miles away during this time of year to either more secure cover or a better food source.

**Shed hunting
will show you what bucks survived the season.**

Supplemental Feeding and Cameras

The best way of proving what animals truly exist in your area is to create a food source that they prefer. Then place a scouting camera at this food source to monitor deer activity.

If it is legal in your state, this is how it is done. During the late winter months, whitetails need food to survive, but their choices are limited. What you should do is provide one feeding station per forty acres or more. Do not put multiple feeding stations on less than forty acres. This will allow the deer too many choices, and you will then need more cameras. You can use shelled corn mixed with molasses that you can buy at a bulk food store. The sweet smell of the molasses will help deer find your food source faster. There are also many commercial deer feeds on the market that are better for the deer than corn. If you do not let your feeding station go empty, you will hold deer on your property that you may not have otherwise.

Once the deer have become accustomed to your food source and are hitting it regularly, it is time to place a scouting camera at the site. Scouting cameras are fairly expensive but are worth every penny. You will only need to place the camera at the feeding site for two weeks. During this period every whitetail, including every mature buck within forty to eighty acres, will have visited your food source. Once caught on film, you will know exactly every mature buck on your property, and what they might score next fall. You might also be able to tell when they have dropped their antlers, and know exactly when to hunt for their sheds. Usually these sheds will then be concentrated by your food source and easier to find. You will quickly become addicted to these cameras, as every time you develop your film it will be just like Christmas!

One last thought. If you are afraid of camera theft, you can place your camera out in the evening and then retrieve it early in the morning each day. Most mature bucks will only be caught on film after dark anyways.

Grow Your Own Monster Whitetails

February is the time that nature decides what a whitetail buck's rack will look like next fall. It is a buck's health condition now that will determine his growth rate this summer. As soon as whitetail bucks drop their antlers they begin the antler growth cycle again. We can help this growth cycle along to grow even bigger and better bucks.

Post Season

Minerals early in the year can help grow bucks like this.

By using supplemental feeding at this time of year, and the use of mineral licks, we can improve the chance of your bucks growing better racks. Minerals like 30-06 or 30-06 with protein made by the Whitetail Institute seem to work well. They additionally have some new products that can be used at different times of the year when the bucks need certain minerals more. These minerals have proven themselves to grow better racks on whitetails. Do not wait until late summer or fall to use them, as the bucks need these nutrients now, and through the spring and summer growing season.

Do not procrastinate!! Now is the time to plan your harvest of mature monster bucks!! Do not wait until late summer or fall to think about deer hunting, or you will find yourself always one step behind that trophy of a lifetime.

Last but not least, remember now is the time to start thinking of equipment changes, not one week before the open season. If you are going to change to a new piece of equipment, now is the time to work the bugs out.

Chapter 3

Spring

March, April, and May are great months to be outdoors. You learned in the last chapter all of those great ways to locate places you would like to hunt. Hopefully you have received your maps, plat books, and aerial photos. You have spent hours going over every inch of information. You now are excited because you can't believe all of the places that you found, and never had thought of before.

After walking all of your existing hunting properties you can't believe how easy it was to locate all of the best stand sites at this time of year. The funnels popped out at you. The bedding areas were easy to find. Trails showed up like roads on a map. Rubs and scrapes were all in the open to see. You may even have found a shed or two. You are pumped for this coming season.

This all sounds great, but there are a couple of problems. No one has ever shown you how to approach these landowners with even a slight chance of getting permission to hunt. Furthermore, now that you know the layout of your existing hunting properties so well, what do you do with them to prepare for the upcoming season?

Never fear, as this is one of the first books that will not only show you what to do in the spring on your existing properties, but will as well show you how to up the odds on getting permission to hunt new ones. This is a very important step in your trophy hunting. If you cannot get permission to hunt the best places where trophy bucks live, all of the other information in this book will do you no good.

Getting proper permission will put you on bucks like this.

Asking Permission

Please follow what you learn here to the letter. You will be amazed at how many places you will get permission to hunt. Places that no one else ever seems to be able to get permission to hunt. Your friends will tell you that you have the golden tongue. You will be seeing and hunting some of the largest bucks in your state. Just follow this simple strategy.

Take a day and drive around the area you are trying to hunt. By using your plat books and aerial photos, locate the properties you are interested in. Then locate the landowners' houses by using the techniques you learned in chapter two. Mark their names and location of their houses on your maps. After you have located all of these landowners, it is time to approach them for permission to hunt.

Approach landowners properly and this can be your reward.

Always approach landowners on beautiful sunny days. This is very important, as most landowners are not as receptive on cold, rainy days, just like you. Pick a day when the temperature is nice, the sun is out, the birds are singing, and the flowers are blooming. These are the days that everyone is in a good mood. Just this one fact will help put the odds in your favor.

**It is what you do now
that will bring you success.**

Pull up to the landowner's house in a clean vehicle. This indicates that you take care of your property and will probably take care of the landowner's as well. Driving an American-made vehicle usually helps also, as most farmers are very pro American. Most trophy hunters know this and will not buy a foreign vehicle because of this fact.

Never pull up in anyone's driveway with anyone in your vehicle, unless it is your wife, your husband, your child, or your one and only hunting partner. Landowners do not like groups of hunters, but do seem to like it if you are a family man or woman. It is usually best if you go by yourself, but if someone else is with you, make sure they get out of the vehicle and approach the landowner with you.

Always approach the side or back door of the landowner's house. This is important, as this is where friends come in. If you look, you will see that many farmhouses have their front door sealed shut and blocked up to keep the weather out. To approach these doors and try to get the homeowner to open them is usually a mistake. If the landowner is in the barn, do not feel afraid to go in and talk to them. This shows you are friendly. To stand outside and call to them will make them uncomfortable.

Wear clean jeans and clean shirts without any offensive slogans on them. Flannel or plaid cotton shirts and clean work boots show that you are not afraid of work and are able to get off the pavement. Clean clothes, and a clean haircut and shave, shows the landowner that you take care of yourself and your things. Do not wear any camouflage clothing, as this is usually a mistake. The only proper time to wear camouflage clothing is when you are hunting.

You will find that it helps to wear a white or light colored baseball cap. It likewise helps if it has a farm slogan on it like "John Deere." The property owners want to know that you understand their way of life, and that you are not just another city slicker. White hats mean you are a good guy.

Approach the property owner with your plat book and aerial photo in hand. This shows you are serious about your hobby of hunting mature whitetails. Show the landowner you know their land and its boundaries. If the landowner was hard to find or does not live on the land you are trying to get permission to hunt, show them how you found them. This may impress them and get you a foot in the door.

If you hunt other farms in the area, do not be afraid to drop names. Most landowners feel better if one of their neighbors think well enough about you to let you hunt their properties. Make friends with the landowner.

If you are a member of the Farm Bureau, let the landowner know. This is a great way to show that you understand the country way of life, and that you belong.

Only ask permission for yourself, or yourself and your wife or child. If your one and only hunting partner is with

Treat landowners with respect and doors will open.

you, and you ask permission for both of you, explain that you hunt with one person for safety reasons. Most property owners will respect this. Tell the landowner that this is your only hunting partner and that you will never bring anyone else on his or her property.

You will find if you ask for permission to bow hunt only more doors will open. Most landowners do not like gun hunters, but will tolerate bow hunters. Later when you become closer friends, they may allow you to gun hunt.

If you get permission to hunt, always ask the landowner where you should park. This shows respect of their property. Tell the landowners that if they give you permission to drive your vehicle across their property to set stands, get a deer out, etc., that you will always ask permission first.

If the landowner says that they have other hunters on their property, please tell them thanks for their time but you do not want to encroach on other hunters. You will find that you really do not want to hunt property with pressure from other hunters. You furthermore would not like someone honing in on your hunting properties. Show other hunters some respect, and hopefully they will show you the same.

Before you leave, whether you get permission or not, ask the landowner if they know of anyone else that may give you permission to hunt. Have them show you on your photos and maps. You may get a surprise and gain access to another hot property for trophy bucks.

Last, but not least, never show anyone else where you hunt. This can create many problems. Once you begin to bring home trophy bucks, everyone will want to know where you hunt. This will have people knocking on your landowners' doors and creating problems. They may even gain permission and push you out of one of your hot spots.

By following the above steps, you will be much closer to finding a spot to hunt with giant bucks walking in front of your stands. Next, you will learn a few other tips that may get you permission to hunt some great properties.

**This buck was taken by
getting permission on only five acres.**

Farm Bureau

Join the Farm Bureau. The cost is usually less than fifty dollars per year. This is a great way to locate help in finding property to hunt. You can find your local Farm Bureau on the Internet or in the yellow pages. The people there are great people, and, if you ask, they may give you some good leads on property to hunt. They are also a good source for plat books and aerial photographs. Most have a bulletin board where you can post an ad showing what you are looking for. Every farmer in the area will walk by this board and look at it.

When you travel to other counties or states, the local Farm Bureau can be a great help. By showing that you are a member, it can open many doors for you. Being a member, once again, shows you understand the country way of life.

Grain Elevators

This is a little-known secret that may help you find property to hunt. Go to the local grain elevators and talk to the people there. They know every farmer in the area. They also usually have a bulletin board where you might be able to post an ad for property to hunt. Plus, you can offer a small reward to the workers at the elevator; if they can find you a farm to hunt that will meet your specifications. Keep in mind to treat these people in a friendly manner, as they can open many doors for you.

Breakfast and Lunch

You are probably thinking, what does this have to do with what we are talking about? Everything that you do to put the odds in your favor might help you gain permission to the best hunting in your life. If you use your imagination anything is possible.

Eating at small local diners can get you information leading to bucks like this.

Every small country town has a local diner where the local farmers hang out. In your travels, while looking for property to hunt in the area, stop in one of these diners and have breakfast or lunch. Usually you will see one big table where all the local farmers sit, drink coffee, and discuss the world's issues.

Take your maps and photographs in with you. Sit near the table that the locals are sitting at. It is usually fairly easy to start a conversation about what you are doing, and these people are great contacts. You may get a big surprise, and one or more of them may just tell you to come out to their place and thin the deer herd out for them.

Controlled Hunts and Out of State Tags

Spring is the time when you should apply for your controlled hunt permits and out of state tags, if you plan on traveling to hunt.

Controlled Hunts usually are hunts that are set up by your state Department of Natural Resources or Federal Wildlife Agencies. These hunts usually take place on state wildlife areas, federal wildlife areas, nature preserves, and military bases that are normally closed to hunting. These places harbor some great bucks.

To get drawn to hunt one of these areas can put you in front of the biggest buck of your life. Look up your Department of Natural Resources on the Internet, and they should supply you with the rules and regulations to apply for the controlled hunts in your state.

If you do get lucky enough to get drawn for a buck tag for one of these hunts, use the resources you learned about in chapter two to get all of the information you need for the area you are hunting. Also, another little-known fact is that most states post a list of people who have been drawn for each hunt. Many of these people have their limit of deer for the season before these hunts get underway. Most of these permits are transferable. If you contact the people on the list, you may get lucky, and one of them may give you their permit.

This buck was taken on a controlled hunt.

Also, early spring is the time you must apply for most out-of-state tags. Make sure you keep up on each state's regulations so that you do not miss their deadlines. You can find the rules and regulations for each state, if you look up their Department of Natural Resources on the Internet.

Next we will look at what other things you should do in the spring to prepare for the upcoming hunting season. These are things we should do on your existing hunting properties. There are many good books and articles written on most of these subjects. We will only lightly touch on them because this book is not about repeating the same information that you read over and over again in other formats. In the next chapter, there will be a list of great books to read on these subjects.

Food Plots

Recall the rules of food, water, and cover. If the landowner allows it, this is the time of year to establish food plots on your properties. Try to keep them small and they will work better. A couple of small food plots are better that one big one. Try to keep these closer to the center of your property, so that the deer travel inward, and the neighbors do not see these animals on your plots. Think of how the deer travel from their bedding areas to the food. Then place your food plots so that the deer must travel through some kind of funnel to get to them. You should think of your property as if you were creating a golf course. Then set up everything to control the movement of the animals. Please read the last two lines again as they are very important.

Water

If water on your property is scarce, you may have to create a water hole. The lack of water is what makes many good looking properties almost barren of deer. It does not take much water to satisfy a whitetail. You can install some kind of water tank, create a pond, or just dig a couple of

Water was the key to this buck.

holes that can hold water for some time. Spring is the time to make this happen. You will as well find that during the rut in the fall, small water holes attract bucks that are thirsty from chasing does. These are great places for stands.

Cover

This is the time of year to create bedding cover, if you need it. If you have a choice, bedding areas should be created close to your property lines. This thick cover will deter the neighbors from crossing over and hunting the wrong side of the fence. Additionally, this makes the animals travel from the outside of your property to the food plots near the center. Please, only do this on property that you own or with permission from the landowner.

It is fairly simple to create a bedding area. First decide where you want to build it, and how large you want to make it. Think again how deer will enter and leave the cover. Take a chain saw and cut two thirds of the way through any tree in the bedding area. Make this cut about four feet off the ground. When the tree falls over leave the trunk attached and it will continue to grow and provide cover and food. Try not to cut down good fruit-bearing trees. Cut every other tree in the area in this manner. Keep cutting until you ask yourself if you have destroyed this part of your property. Then continue to cut for one hour more.

The cover you have created will look terrible at first. But do not fear. As sunlight gains access to the ground, this area will grow into a beautiful, thick bedding area.

Funnels

Now is the time of year to find or create funnels. These are what you might call pinch points, which deer are forced to travel through. Deer must travel to get from bedding cover to food and/or water. Bucks furthermore travel a lot during rut from one bedding area to the next. Hopefully,

This barn and field creates a perfect funnel.

you have a good understanding of most common funnels. The concept of hunting funnels could fill a book all by itself. If you would like to learn more about hunting funnels, the books listed in the following chapter will explain this concept in detail. There are a couple of ideas you should be aware of though.

Never be afraid of creating your own funnels. You should think of your hunting properties as golf courses. If you have learned anything from the first chapter, you might even be hunting a golf course. Besides this fact, you should think of controlling every movement of your deer herd. This is much better than chasing them around haphazard-like. Use your imagination.

Block trails that you do not want deer to use. Brush, fencing, downed trees, or anything else you can think of will work. Open up any places you would like the deer to travel through. Mow lanes, trim brush, or cut trails through the thickets. Any large area that is too wide to hunt effectively can be closed up with some sort of fence built with either wire or brush and downed trees. Think about forcing the deer to travel where the wind is correct for you to hunt that spot.

Always keep your mind open. Houses, barns, old cars, livestock fences, junk piles, and sand pits are just a few things that can alter a buck's travel pattern. These things could direct a monster buck right to your tree stand. A few man-made funnels can make a mediocre property into a great one.

One last, and final, thought on the subject of funnels. The more man encroaches on the whitetails' world, the more funnels are created. Some things that may seem terrible at the time may be blessings in disguise. Always think positive. This gives the smart hunter better odds on taking a mature buck.

Tree Stands

Spring is the time when you should preset any stands on your existing properties. You may have to wait until the fall to set some stands, but any time you can do it in the

Now is the time to set stands.

spring will usually give you a better chance to be on target. Everything will look just like it does during the late fall.

It is easy at this time of year to see how much cover is in the tree to hide a hunter. You should temporarily set your stands so that you may trim all of your shooting lanes now. Just cut them a little wider than you would in the fall, and by the time summer growing season is over they will be perfect. There are usually no or very few leaves on the branches at this time of year; therefore, you should not have to drag them away.

You do not have to worry about leaving scent behind or disturbing the deer at this time of year. Once you have detailed each stand, you can remove them until fall. Then you only have to slip in and quietly replace them, and you are ready to hunt with minimal disturbance.

There is an art form to setting and placing stands. This is very important, as you will spend many hours in them. In chapter six you will learn in detail how to set and approach your stands.

This buck was the result of spring planning.

Chapter 4

Summer

You are probably wondering what you can do during the months of June, July, and August to help improve your odds in hunting monster bucks. Most people would say nothing, but they would be wrong. Any true trophy whitetail hunter can always find something to do, almost any time of the year, to help them get closer to their goals. Summer is no exception.

Family

One of the most important things in your quest for trophy whitetails is a very understanding family. Without the support of your loved ones, you may never have the drive and motivation to be successful in your passion.

Summer is the time to show your gratitude for being gone so much during the hunting season. Spend the summer with your family on vacation. Take your spouse or sweetheart, if you have one, out on dates. Take the kids to the movies or to a baseball game. Try to do anything fun with your family that does not have to do with hunting. These things will bring good memories for both you and your family. You will think of these great memories in the fall when you are out sitting in your treestand.

Mow the grass, wash the cars, work on the house, and do the chores. Take the time to be responsible for the other things in your life. Summer is the time for you and the deer to rest and rejuvenate before the action-packed fall hunting season.

Spend time with your family during the summer and then you will enjoy hunting in the fall.

Scouting

Many authors write about watching bean fields, other crops, and food plots during the summer for bachelor groups of bucks. Bucks will group together during the summer months. Many of these bucks will lie out in the fields, in the shade, while their racks grow. They are very visible, as at this time of year they may be out very early in the evening feeding in the fields.

In the new world of hunting trophy bucks in highly pressured areas, watching them in the summer is normally not a good idea. The reason is that if you are watching a big buck out in the field, there is a high probability someone else is as well. Drawing attention to these trophy animals is not a good idea. If someone sees your truck parked along the road, with you watching with a pair of binoculars, they will get curious and want to know what you are looking at. The news of a sighting of a big buck travels fast. Soon many people may be watching.

Some people are not as ethical as you are, and your wonderful find may not live long enough until the season starts. Plus, you will find many people knocking on your landowner's door trying to get permission to hunt the property. They might just gain total control of the property, leaving you looking from the outside in.

There is one other good reason not to scout or bother your deer herd during the summer months. During the spring and summer, a trophy buck's rack is growing many inches per week. During this intense growing time, his rack is composed of thousands of soft blood vessels. This makes his rack very susceptible to damage.

If you were to any way chase or force a big buck to run for cover, he may easily damage his rack by hitting a tree, a fence, or any other hard object. Once his rack is damaged during the growing period it loses the memory of the part that was damaged. If he breaks a part of his rack after it hardens in the fall, he will not lose memory, and he will grow the same rack next year, but only larger until his declining years, if he lives that long. This damage, during the growing period of his rack, is why there are so many whitetails in areas of high human population and hunting

The smart hunter does not bother the deer during the summer months.

pressure that have only a half rack or their rack scores so poorly due to damage. As you already know, any mature buck is a trophy, but you should want him to score at his highest potential. This is the time to stay out of the woods.

Practice Shooting

Summer is the time to practice shooting, not just one week before you go hunting. Take a little time every week and practice with your bow, rifle, shotgun, or muzzleloader. This is the time to make any changes to your equipment. This will work the bugs out, and help build any muscles or coordination necessary to shoot your equipment.

There is nothing worse than going through all the work and having a monster buck standing in front of you, only to not be able to hit the mark and take him home. This book is about odds, and having the ability to hit what you're aiming at will up your odds greatly in your search for that trophy.

Those last couple of paragraphs may be small but they are very important. Please learn to shoot your equipment properly. In chapter eight you will learn about the proper weapons to get the job done.

Get Equipment Ready

Do not wait until just before the season to get all of your hunting equipment ready. Summer is the time to repair and paint your treestands, organize your gear, and buy anything that you lost or broke last season. Many hunters wait until just before the season to buy the things they need. Many sporting goods stores are out of the things you need by then. Most of the best hunting clothing is gone before the hunting season. Do not procrastinate, but buy your items early.

In chapter seven you will learn about some of the items that are priceless in the woods. Many of these items will greatly up the odds in your quest for that trophy whitetail.

Summer is for practice.

Get In Shape

Many people think that it is relaxing and easy to quietly sit in a treestand and wait for a poor, unsuspecting deer to walk by. They are terribly wrong. You need to be in shape to sit for many hours in a tree, especially if you sit from daylight to dark during the rut. The swaying of your tree from the wind will constantly use every muscle in your body to keep balance. If you are out of shape you will lose concentration quickly.

Walking around in rough and hilly terrain likewise is demanding. Try dragging a two hundred pound deer for a long ways back to the vehicle. Long hours without sleep will furthermore drain your energy, if you are not in shape. Setting multiple stands in the spring or fall takes a person who is in good physical condition. Otherwise it can get dangerous if you tire quickly. Just climbing into your stand in the morning or back down in the evening takes good balance and strong muscles, if you are to be safe.

Summer is the time to get back in shape, if you have to. Take long walks with your spouse to increase stamina. Do some weight training. Go on that diet that we all hate. Lose those extra pounds that you do not want to carry up that tree or over that hill during the hunting season.

Here is one good excuse to go fishing. The movement of a boat in the wind and waves closely simulates the movement of a tree in the wind. This will help in building the muscles necessary to be comfortable for hours in a tree. I bet you never thought of that one before.

Set Your Calendar

Now is the time to plan all of the dates that you will be hunting. In the process of putting all of the odds in your favor, you will find that it is better to hunt when the mature bucks are most active during daylight hours, than just to hunt as much as you can. During some of the following chapters you will learn the peak times to hunt. These times will be when the mature bucks are most vulnerable and

You need to get in shape to last the long season.

moving during daylight hours. If you are limited in the time you have to hunt, by scheduling your hunting times around certain dates, you can greatly up your odds.

By using your guides to the state regulations and hunting seasons, you can also plan the best times to hunt with different weapons. By comparing hunting seasons between your state and any neighboring states, you will be in the woods at the proper times with the best weapon you can use during those times. For example, if in one state it is late archery season, and in your neighboring state it is muzzleloader season, you can up your reach and odds by hunting with your muzzleloader.

Hunting Partners

Your hunting partner, good or bad, will usually determine whether you will be a successful trophy hunter or not. Many trophy hunters hunt alone due to the fact that it is hard to find a good hunting partner. This allows them to do what they have to do without any restrictions. Hunting alone means having all of your best spots to yourself. Anytime only one person enters the woods, they will only leave half as much scent on the ground as would two people in the same woods.

To have three or more hunting partners is probably not a good idea either. Any time there are more than two people hunting any one area, the odds of one of them taking home a monster buck lowers dramatically. Groups of people hunting on small, highly pressured areas are usually a mistake that cannot be fixed.

If you have a bad or indifferent hunting partner you should think of moving on if you want to be successful at trophy hunting. Anyone who does not show up on time in the morning, or is not ready and waiting for you when you pick them up, should be avoided. If you find yourself always doing all of the work for both of you, it is time to move on. If your partner is always in a negative mood and does not push you to keep going, you are better off without them.

A good hunting partner makes all the difference.

Never settle and hunt with someone who does not bring something positive to the party.

A great hunting partner will always make sure you get up in time in the early hours of the morning. They will always share in all of the tasks that lead to that monster buck. A great hunting partner doubles the odds that at least one of you will take home a trophy whitetail every season. This type of hunting partner is always willing to learn and is always willing to try something new. They will work as hard trying to get you your buck as they do trying to get their own.

If you do not like hunting alone find yourself a good hunting partner. Do not settle for second best, as you will always be disappointed. Do not feel guilty if you tell your present hunting partner that you are no longer going to hunt with them. This is for the best if you truly want to hunt mature bucks. It is as hard to find a good hunting partner, as it is to find good hunting property.

Just because you find someone who shares your desire to hunt trophy bucks, you do not have to hunt the same properties. They can help you set up your properties, and you can help them do the same. Then when it is time to hunt, you both can go your separate ways. At the end of each hunt, you can compare notes and give each other ideas on how to turn the odds more in your favor. This works well in many cases.

If you can find a great hunting partner, and you both decide to hunt the same properties, you are very lucky. Any time you can cover more than one direction that a mature buck might travel, you have doubled your odds of one of you getting a chance at him. You will know when you find this kind of hunting partner, as you will not be afraid if they sit in one of your best stands. You know they will be as careful as yourself, and the deer will not know they were even there. You will both feed off each other, and even though you think the same, you both will have different ideas on how to handle each situation that you are confronted with.

Talking about hunting partners in a chapter about what to do during the summer may sound funny, but if you can find someone who is fired up about big bucks at this time of year, you may have found someone that could be the hunting partner you are looking for.

This is the time to forget about last season's problems and to find someone that will help make this season one to remember. If you go forward with a positive mind, you will put the odds in your favor.

Learning the truth about hunting pressured bucks is what it is all about.

Books to Read

No one should ever consider himself or herself the only authority on hunting mature whitetails. Hopefully you will consider this book the ultimate guide on hunting mature bucks in highly pressured areas, but many things can be learned from other great hunting authors. Below is a great list of books on hunting trophy whitetails. You should spend the summer reading some of them. If you do, your understanding of mature whitetails, their habits, and hunting strategies for them, will increase. All of these authors are true hunters, and not just writers looking to make a buck.

These books are in no particular order:

- Hunting Hard for Whitetails – Bill Winke – Derrydale Press.

- Treestand Strategies – Gene & Barry Wensel – Derrydale Press

- Advanced Scouting for Whitetails - Judd Cooney – Derrydale Press.

- Locating Trophy Whitetails – David Morris - Derrydale Press.

- Taking Trophy Whitetails – Bob Fratzke - Target Communications.

- Moonstruck – Jeff Murray – Full Moon Press.

- Hunting Whitetails by the Moon – Charles J. Alsheimer – Krause Publications.

- Aggressive Whitetail Hunting - Greg Miller – Krause Publications.

- Hunting Rutting Whitetails – Gene Wensel.

- One Man's Whitetail - Gene Wensel.

- The Art & Science of Patterning Whitetails – Dr. James C. Kroll – Gordon Whittington.

- Bowhunting's Whitetail Masters – Dan Bertalan – Envisage Unlimited.

- Relentless Pursuit – Tim Wells – World Hunting Group Publishers Company.

- Hunting Trophy Whitetails – David Morris – Venture Press.

- Advanced Strategies for Trophy Whitetails – David Morris – Safari Press.

- Mapping Trophy Bucks – Brad Herndon – Krause Publications.

Chapter 5

Pre-season

September is the month that is usually considered pre-season. This is when the excitement of the coming hunting season starts to take over. The temperature outside starts to cool down and the feeling of fall is in the air. Hunting magazines begin to show up on the shelves. Hunting shows can be watched in the mornings on the weekends. You start watching all of your old deer hunting videos, and pick up any new ones you find. Your passion for deer hunting pops up in all of your conversations with your friends.

This is the time of year when you realize that all of the work you did in the spring is about to pay off soon. The average hunter is lost at this time of year, as he still has not gone out and made an attempt to acquire a place to hunt this year. You, on the other hand, feel confident as you have already scouted your existing properties in the spring, and have picked up a couple of new hot spots earlier in the year. There are only a few things left to do before it is time to hunt that trophy whitetail.

Visit Your Landowners

Take the time before the hunting season starts and visit the great people that have given you permission to hunt this season. Reassure them that you are ethical and will not damage their property. Ask if anything has changed since you last visited. Sometimes you may find that they have sold some of their property or have purchased some new property that you can hunt. You should further find out if they have changed anything on their property, such as logging or creating a pond. Check and see if they plan on doing anything in the fall that may interfere with the deer or your hunting.

One of the most important things about this visit is to find out if the landowner has given permission to any other hunters this season. Pressure from other hunters is the most damaging thing that will keep you from getting that trophy buck more than anything else. By showing up at the landowner's door shows that you are still interested in spending time on their property, and they are more likely to say no to the last-minute hunters knocking at their door.

Pressure from other hunters is the number one reason to make you look elsewhere for better hunting opportunities. You do not have any control over the other hunters' actions, and those trophy bucks catch on quick that they are being hunted. Then they become almost impossible to kill.

Hunting Equipment

This is the time to make sure all of your hunting equipment is ready. Do not wait until the last minute, or it could cost you your one and only chance at that trophy buck this season. This book is about putting all of the odds in your favor, and having all of your equipment ready and in good working order, as a big part of helping your odds.

Organize your equipment so that you can take inventory of what you have and what you are missing. Every little detail counts. Don't forget to get your hunting vehicle in perfect working order, too. There is nothing worse than knowing the rut is in full swing but your vehicle is in the shop and you cannot get into the field.

In the rest of this chapter, and the following few chapters, we will discuss the different types of equipment to use to put the odds in your favor, and to get you close to that monster buck you have always dreamed about.

If your equipment is ready your odds of taking home a buck like this greatly increases.

Tree Stands

There are only a few great hunters that can claim success at taking huge whitetails from the ground. It is very difficult for most hunters to get a chance at a mature buck from the ground unless you are using a long-range weapon. This fact forces most hunters to rely on some type of elevated tree stand to help put the odds in their favor of getting close to a big buck.

There are many models of tree stands on the market, but really only a few different types. The different types are defined as ladder stands, climbing stands, fixed position stands, and the tree sling or saddle stand. When deciding on which stands you want to use for hunting recognize that the more simply a stand is built, the better it is usually to hunt from. Also try to restrict yourself to one or two models of each type of tree stand you choose. This leads to familiarity in each stand, which helps in ease of setting them, and in being comfortable to you when in use. Let's look at each of these stands one at a time and explain their uses and differences.

Ladder stands are usually the most simple and usually the safest type of tree stand. The downfall is that this type of stand is the least versatile of the different types of stands. Usually they are very heavy and cumbersome, making setting or moving them a chore. Ladder stands stand out in the woods like a sore thumb alerting the more mature deer, and they are very visible to other hunters. With a ladder stand you are restricted to a certain height to hunt from.

The best places to use this type of tree stand are areas with low hunting pressure or when you are using a long range weapon, so that you do not have to set up too close to the action. Even though ladder stands may not be the best choice, they are usually one step better than hunting from the ground. Ladder stands are a good choice for young hunters to learn from and older hunters who are not comfortable hunting in the air off the ground. The ladder stand is normally a poor choice for the trophy hunter.

These are just half of the tree stands we use.

Climbing tree stands are much more versatile than ladder stands. They are very comfortable to hunt from and today's models are very safe, if used properly. Many of the newer models are very light and are great if you need to move your stand often or you want to quickly set up in an area that you have not previously hunted. These stands make a good bow hunting stand and a great gun hunting stand. One good reason to use a climbing stand is that you always carry it with you, and other hunters will have a hard time finding your stand sites.

The only downfall to the climbing stand is that they must be used in a medium-sized, fairly straight tree, and you are unable to climb past any limbs without cutting them off. They can, however, be used as a fixed position stand if you need to. Most are so comfortable that they are great for all-day hunts. Every true trophy hunter should have at least one climbing stand.

Fixed position tree stands are the most versatile of the tree stand types, which is why they are the most widely used by trophy hunters. With this type of tree stand you must use them with some kind of climbing device, such as tree steps, or climbing sticks. With a fixed position stand you are not restricted to a fixed height or size of tree. You are also able to climb past limbs without cutting them, and this allows them to provide cover.

There are many more models of this type of stand than any other. Once again you should try to restrict yourself to one or two models. Try to use the quietest stand you can find, that moreover has a simple design and is easy to hang. The less moving parts the better. Use high quality screw in steps when possible; unless the laws or the landowner does not allow it, then there are many climbing sticks to choose from.

Finally there is the tree sling or sometimes called the tree saddle. This type of stand is modeled after a lineman's style belt, but more comfortable. They are very lightweight and can be used in any size tree. They likewise must be used with some type of climbing system to get you to the height you would like to hunt. They are your tree stand and safety belt combined. The only downfall to this type of stand is that many hunters feel awkward and uncomfortable using them.

Last, but not least, always use a safety harness or belt when hunting from a tree stand. No animal or trophy is worth injury or your life. There is nothing macho about not wearing one, and you have nothing to prove by doing so. Always keep in mind your family and friends want you to come home from the woods safe and sound.

Permanent Tree Stands

As you have noticed, permanent tree stands were not included in the types of tree stands mentioned above. This type of stand usually has no place in trophy whitetail hunting. These stands are an eye sore, and many times they are unsafe to climb into. After a season or so, the nails in these stands pull out of the tree, and they can be an accident waiting to happen. Most mature deer know that hunters use them, and avoid them completely. Additionally, any other hunter on your property will know where these stands are, and might use them when you are not there.

Setting up Tree Stands

Most of your stands should have been set late in February or early March, but, as you know, we all run late including me. Therefore, September is when most of our stands are being set. If you are one of the late ones, try getting your stands set as early in September as you can. This allows you a couple of weeks for the deer to settle down before your hunt begins.

When setting your stands at this time of year, always trim walking lanes to your stands with a small hand pruner. Most hunters are detected by bucks when they leave scent on leaves and branches as they are coming and going from their stand sites. No matter how short your walk is through the woods to your stands, always trim your path and use some sort of marking method.

Never set stands without a pole pruner.

Small reflective tacks, called bright-eyes, seem to work very well when marking your path to your stands. These markers are almost undetectable by other hunters during the daylight hours. During the dark they brightly show up with your flashlight, keeping you from stepping off your access trail.

If you set stands in the spring, September is the time to check them. Make sure you touch up access trails and shooting lanes altered by summer's plant growth. When you trim around your stands in the spring, cut ample size lanes so that they do not grow shut during the summer growing season. Then by fall they will not be noticed, and you will not have to hardly prune any foliage.

If you are setting your stands in September, make sure to trim small shooting lanes. This is due to the foliage dropping as fall progresses. If you cut large lanes now, they will look like airplane landing fields as the season progresses, and those monster bucks will avoid them.

This is also very important; always use a pole pruner when trimming shooting lanes. There has never been a hunter that could effectively trim shooting lanes without one. Buy one, borrow one, but always use one. If you do not decide to use one, your shooting lanes will look like meadows in the woods. This is due to your cutting small saplings and trees off near the ground, when all you had to do was trim off a small branch or two with a pole pruner. Mature bucks will avoid these areas! Besides, by not using a pole pruner, this will force you to set your stands too low.

There is something else to consider. Always walk right down one of your shooting lanes on the last twenty or twenty-five yards to your stand. This is so that if a mature buck does smell your trail on the way past your stand it will be too late, as he will now be in one of your shooting lanes. How many times has a deer come by your stand and stopped just before entering a shooting lane? This is usually due to the fact that the deer caught scent that you left on the ground or brush as you approached your stand.

Everyone always wants to know how high to set his or her stands. This is usually determined by the amount of background cover you have to work with. Usually in highly pressured hunting areas the higher you go the better. In some of these areas twenty to twenty-five feet to the platform of your stand is the norm.

Make sure you set your stands on the downwind side of where you expect the deer to travel. Never hunt any stand unless the wind is correct for that location. Try not to cross any deer trails to get to your stand, if you can.

Try to set your stands so that the sun is not in your face during the time you are planning to sit in each location. Furthermore, hang a bow or gun rope from each stand so you do not have to set your weapon on the ground before you climb into your stand. Likewise, pull the bottom five steps or so every time you leave your stand. This will deter other hunters from using, or stealing, your stands. Plus, hang and leave a bow or gun hook at each stand. Moreover, these small steps will allow you to climb into your stand, and set up to hunt with very little disturbance.

In the next chapter we will discuss how to approach your stands, and the scent-free, low-profile hunting approach you should use when hunting pressured whitetails.

Game Cameras

Many people like to use game cameras just before the hunting season to try and locate and determine what type of bucks are on their hunting property. There are times when these cameras are great to use, but just before the hunting season is not one of them. In a highly pressured hunting area this is usually a mistake. The disturbance from setting and checking these cameras can pressure a good buck out of the area. The less you disturb the deer at this time of year will improve your odds as the hunting season progresses.

Leave your game cameras at home and you will have a better chance of getting a picture like this.

Checking and Watching Crop Fields

This is the time of year to check all of your properties to see what crops are planted in what fields. This can change your strategy for hunting each property.

Soybeans in a field are a great early and late season food source. They are one of the most preferred foods of the whitetail deer. Most deer will pass up corn for beans if they are available. Likewise, if there are beans in the fields, you then know the deer must be bedding elsewhere in the thickets and woods. This will force the deer to travel within the cover and you can plan your hunting strategy accordingly.

If corn is growing in the fields, it changes everything. Corn is some of the best bedding and security cover a big buck can find. Until the fields are harvested, most mature bucks in a highly pressured hunting area will seldom leave these fields except for water or another food source like acorns or apples. Your hunting strategy on these farms will constantly change as the cornfields become harvested.

Just like we discussed in the last chapter about summer, you should not openly watch those fields for deer in highly pressured areas. You will just tip off other hunters to those giant bucks that you may find. The only time that you should watch those fields for quality animals is a couple of days just before hunting season starts. This may give you one of the best chances to bring home a monster buck each season. You will learn more about this in chapter ten under glassing.

Shooting Broadheads Only

Last, but not least. This is the time of year to practice shooting broadheads only if you are a bowhunter. This will give you the confidence to hit what you are aiming at when that big buck shows up this season. If you only practice with field tips, you are hurting your odds even if they fly just like your broadheads. In the back of your mind you will have some doubt when the time arrives to make that shot count on that monster buck.

Make sure all of your other weapons are sighted in properly also. There is nothing worse than hearing everyone shooting their firearms the day before deer hunting season starts as they sight them in. A big buck that has survived a few seasons knows what all that noise means, and he will head for security before you ever hit the woods.

In the next three chapters we are going to discuss how to approach your stands, and the equipment that you need to hunt those giant bucks close to home in those highly pressured areas.

This is what makes all the planning worthwhile.

Chapter 6

Low Profile Hunting

Before you dive into the hunting season, you must learn a few things to help put all of the odds in your favor. This is very important if you want to have an encounter with that trophy of a lifetime. Low profile hunting should be the number one tactic that all of your other hunting strategies are based on.

In highly pressured areas there are only a few big bucks to go around. If any one of these animals feels that they are being hunted, they will seem to vanish into thin air. The best way to hunt these animals is to never let them know you are there and that they are being hunted. In this chapter, and the following few, you will learn about the equipment and tactics you need to completely hide from your quarry.

Scent Control

Scent, sound, and sight are the whitetail's biggest defenses listed in the order of most importance. A mature buck can keep track of danger by covering a very large area with just his nose alone. Most hunters think that a deer only knows that a human is hunting them if they happen to walk downwind of the hunter's stand and smell them.

What most hunters do not realize is that it is just not the human scent that is traveling on the air currents from their stands that alert the deer. Most whitetails discover that they are being hunted by the odors left behind by the hunter coming and going from his stands. By learning to

No scent is the best scent.

control your scent, you will be one step closer to becoming a ghost as you travel through the woods hunting those monster bucks.

Scent Control Clothing

Scent control clothing came out quite a few years back. Its purpose was to eliminate human scent. Originally only one manufacturer made this type of clothing. Now there are a handful of manufacturers out there producing good quality, scent control clothing.

Many casual hunters feel that this type of clothing does no good at eliminating human scent. What you must know is that this clothing is just part of the system you should use to help eliminate or reduce your human scent in the field. If you do not buy into and use a complete scent control system, you will not contain your scent enough to consistently bring home those monster whitetails.

There is probably not a true trophy hunter out there that does not rely on some type of scent control clothing. It does not really matter which brand of this type of clothing that you buy. The important thing is that you use it properly.

Do not just use the coat and pants of this clothing. You must likewise cover your head, mouth, and even your hands. Make sure you keep this product properly cleaned per the manufacturer's recommendations. Most of this type of clothing gets revitalized, if you put it in the dryer for a period of time. You will find that the more often you do this the better your hunting becomes.

Always store this product and any other equipment in a sealed scent-proof bag or container. Never wear this, or any of your other hunting clothing around fire, gas stations, restaurants, the house, in your car, or anywhere that you could contaminate your clothing with foreign smells that could alert that trophy whitetail to your presence.

Proper scent free clothing is the key.

Laundry Soap

Having good hunting and scent control clothing does no good if you wash it in regular scented laundry detergent. Please make sure you wash everything that you wear into the woods with a scent-free detergent. There are many companies that make detergent especially for hunting clothes. If you do decide to use detergent from the grocery store, there are many that are dye free and scent-free that work great. Just make sure you read the bottle or box.

To skip this step, or any other, in the scent-control system, will greatly lower your odds. You need to go all the way or not at all. Once your clothes are clean and scent free, place them in your scent-free bags or containers. Do not put these clothes on until you are ready to hunt. Plus, make sure that all of the undergarments that you are wearing were washed in the same scent-free soap.

Footwear

No true trophy hunter would be caught without good knee-high, rubber boots. There are many quality brands of boots on the market. It does no good to wear scent-free clothing only to leave human scent all over the ground for deer to smell. This is most important in areas of high hunting pressure.

Never wear your boots unless you are hunting. Keep them clean by washing them with baking soda and water. Then store them in a scent-free bag or container. You will find these boots lose the ability to contain your scent after a couple of seasons and you should replace them.

When you do wear these boots, liberally spray them down with a good scent eliminator spray. Bear in mind, a buck's nose spends most of its time between approximately the height of your waist and then down to the ground. The less scent you leave behind the better. This brings us to our next topic.

Scent control is a total system.

Sprays

Scent eliminating sprays have been very controversial. Some people believe they have no real purpose and are nothing but baking soda and water. Whether this is true or not, you should still use them. There are many scent eliminating sprays on the market. Find one that you feel works best and use it. It cannot hurt, and it is furthermore a great confidence builder as you walk to your stand.

Take the time before you head to your stand and spray down thoroughly. Spray down your outer clothes before you put them on. Spray down your rubber hunting boots and your pants. Spray your hat and backpack. Spray anything that you think you should, and it will improve your confidence while you hunt.

Taking a Shower

Now that everything you wear is totally scent free, why would you wear after-shave into the woods? Hopefully you would not. The cleaner and more scent free you keep your body and hair the better.

Human odor comes from bacteria growing on your body and hair. The more you shower, the better you will control bacteria. Do not be afraid to shower before every hunt, even if that means twice a day for morning and evening hunts.

Make sure you use scent-control soap and shampoo that you can find at better sporting goods stores. Then use a scent free deodorant so that you remain odor free.

Good hygiene is essential to the low profile hunting system. It is one more; very important item that will help put the odds in your favor, so that you can take home that monster buck.

Make sure you shower with scent control soap before every hunt.

Breath Control

Bad breath can ruin your hunt just as fast as anything else. All of the other things that you do to control your odor while sitting in your stand does no good, if you have the breath of a dragon. Never fear because there is a cure for bad breath. Your spouse, family, friends, or significant other will appreciate your new fresh breath as well.

First, buy a tongue scraper from your local drug store. They are relatively inexpensive. Scrape the top of your tongue with this scraper prior to brushing your teeth.

Next, make a mouthwash solution of half 3% hydrogen peroxide and half salty water. Please make sure the hydrogen peroxide is 3%. Hydrogen peroxide usually costs only a dollar per bottle, which you can find at your local drug store. Gargle with this solution for at least a couple of minutes. Spit the solution out and rinse with plain water. Do not swallow this solution.

Finally make a tooth powder out of a combination of three parts baking soda and one part salt. Mix this thoroughly and store in a dry container. Use this tooth powder on a wet toothbrush. Then gently brush your teeth, gums, tongue, and every part of your mouth. Do this for at least a couple of minutes. After a week or so you should find that you have no breath odor.

Controlling Bad Odors

There are many odors out there that can ruin your hunt for that trophy buck. The more you think about them, and avoid them, the better your odds of taking home that trophy whitetail.

If you have pets, try to keep your equipment away from them and where they lay. Do not stop at the gas station on the way to your hunt. Do not eat breakfast or lunch in your hunting clothes. If you are setting stands at the last minute or dragging and cleaning a deer, please wear clothes other than your hunting clothes, and take a shower before going back into the woods.

You are probably able to think of many other odors that may ruin your hunt. Keep this in mind, and you will be successful in your trophy hunting.

Wind Direction

Many articles and books are written about using the wind in your favor. They go into great detail and should be studied. Many of the suggested books in chapter four go into great depths on the subject. You should be familiar with the subject, if you have deer hunted at all. By now you should have a good understanding about the use of the wind and air currents, but there are a couple of things that should never leave your mind.

Never hunt a stand if the wind is not in your favor. Pressured bucks do not make mistakes after they have survived a couple of years. To let them locate you in your stand, just once, will make that stand useless.

When you are preparing your stands, always keep wind direction in mind. If you are creating funnels or controlling deer movement in any way, make the deer move to a stand where the wind is in your favor.

Scent-control clothing and hygiene is not always perfect, and do not just rely on it when hunting mature whitetails. You must use everything you can to gain an advantage. This is how you put the odds in your favor to take home that monster buck.

When entering and leaving your stand, always think of where your scent is blowing as you travel through the woods. It does no good to let the deer know your location, even when you are not hunting and just traveling to and from your stand. This brings us to our next subject.

**Even with scent control
never hunt when the wind is wrong.**

Stand Approach

Stand approach is the most overlooked subject of deer hunting. How you enter and leave your stands is vital, if you ever want to have a chance at getting a shot at that trophy of a lifetime. If you cannot get to or from a stand without alerting your deer, that stand is useless.

Always set your stands using the guidelines set forth in the last chapter. Use those bright eyes so you know exactly where you are walking, and, therefore, you do not touch any branches, as you have trimmed them with your hand pruner in advance. The following few subjects will explain how to approach your stands.

Where to Park

A mature buck keeps tabs on everything it hears up to a mile from where it is at all times. Just like a young child, when they are fawns they only pay attention to things going on within a couple of yards. As they become yearlings, they may keep track of a hundred yards or so. From a year and a half to two and a half years of age, they are aware of anything they hear up to a couple hundred yards away. Finally after they mature, they will take notice of anything within a square mile.

One big mistake made by most hunters is to park along side the road or in a lane where seldom anyone parks. This is very disturbing to a mature buck, and he will take evasive action immediately. Most hunters are not aware this is even happening while they sit in their car having coffee or getting ready for the day's hunt.

Always try to park at the landowner's house or barn area. Deer hear cars coming and going from these properties all of the time and pay little attention, as this seems natural to them. If you need to park at a different spot on the property to get to your stands, try to park in a low profile spot where it is hard for the deer to hear you pull over. Then quietly as possible exit your vehicle.

One great trick is to ask the closest neighbor if you can park at their house, even if you do not hunt their property. You will be surprised that most do not mind, and you may even make a friend that might open doors to more great hunting property.

The more you act like a resident landowner the less the deer will feel you are a threat. Besides by parking at someone's house or barn, other hunters will have a harder time noticing that you are hunting the area. Remember, low profile hunting!!

Do Not Be Seen

Most people do not realize that more hunters are probably seen or heard while going to and coming from their stands by deer, than ever located by those same whitetails once they are in their stands. Getting from your vehicle to your stand is as important as the stand placement itself.

Early in the season you may be able to get away with a few things due to the fact that the foliage is thick and lush. After leaf drop the woods open up and the deer can see your movement from a long ways.

Always use the cover and terrain to your advantage as you walk to your stand. Never walk across an open field, or where you can be sky lined, especially if you think the deer have a chance of spotting you. Think of how the deer gets from point A to point B without ever being seen. If you use the same principles, you will be amazed how you can get through the woods to your stand without alerting any of the deer herd.

Going In Early vs. Going In Late

There are many opinions about whether going to your stand early in the dark or waiting until daylight to go to your stand in the morning is the right thing to do. Every stand and time of the year is different, but here are a few guidelines.

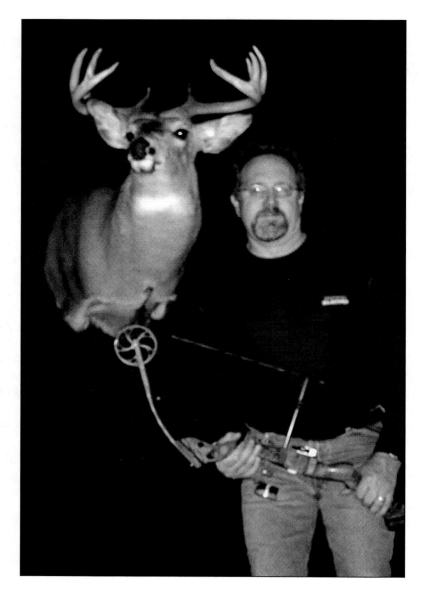

You must get to and from your stand without the deer knowing.

Normally, if you go to your stand just before daylight, it is the wrong thing to do. If you are trying to beat a monster buck to his bedding area, you should be there more than an hour before daylight. Likewise, if you are hunting a small woodlot out in the middle of an open field, you should be in place more than an hour before daylight. If you get there late, the deer will already be in the woodlot, and you will chase them out the other side. You will not even know it happened. If you are late walking across the field in the dark, the deer will be in the field with you, and, as they watch you go to the woodlot, they will go elsewhere. Once again you will never know they were there.

If you are hunting funnels, especially during the rut, and have to cross open fields where the deer spend the night, you may opt to wait until the deer enter the woods in the morning after daylight. Then you can see across the open fields while you work your way to your stand. The deer usually bed down just at daylight near the field edges just inside the woods. Then they get moving again an hour or so later, as they move towards bedding areas. By then you will be in your stand waiting for them.

One excellent trick to use is to go in very early to hunt a small woodlot. If the deer do not show up within an hour after daylight, you should figure they are not coming. You should get down from your stand at this time and move towards one of your stands in the larger timber that you could not get to in the dark. This trick alone can double your productive hunting time in the morning, putting more of the odds in your favor.

Raking Paths

One trick many trophy hunters use to quietly approach their stands is to rake the ground bare for the last fifty yards or more to each stand. This makes for a very quiet entrance and exit from each stand location.

If you decide to do this, you will find that you must rake each location at least twice per season. You must do this once before leaf drop, and at least once or twice after leaf drop. This is a lot of work, and it will create quite a disturbance each time you do this. Mature bucks in highly pressured areas may not tolerate the intrusion.

One other problem is that if you decide to rake paths to your stands, you must make sure it is on properties where no other people are hunting. This is due to the fact that these trails are easy to find, and the other hunters will know where you are hunting.

Act Like a Squirrel

Another option to stand approach is to act like another small animal in the woods. The trick to this is not to walk steady, or to take a few steps, then stop without making noise for a moment. These are the sounds of a predator. Deer will key in on these sounds.

If you have ever listened to the squirrels in the woods, you know that they take a few jumps, and then dig around in the leaves, and then they take a few more jumps, and dig in the leaves again. These little animals are always in motion, and make a lot of noise for their size. Deer take this noise for granted, and pay almost no attention to it.

When approaching your stands, take three steps and then stop. Take your foot or a branch, and continue to make noise in the leaves on the ground. Repeat this process all the way to your stand. The deer will pay little attention to the noise you make. Then when you climb into your tree, the small noises you make against the bark will be just written off as another squirrel.

This may sound funny, but try it once and you will see the difference it makes.

Run to Your Stands

Even funnier is the concept of running to your stand. When the woods are so crunchy from frost or dry leaves that you sound like an elephant going to your stand, this may be an option you should try.

This buck was fooled by Mark running to his stand.

Deer are spooked constantly and can be heard running through the woods. This is especially true during the rut. If you run the last fifty yards or more to your stand, the deer will definitely hear you. You will find that they will quickly regard you as just another spooked deer in the woods. The trick is once you get to your stand, to stand still for about five minutes before you climb into your tree. This will allow the deer that did take notice of your loud display to calm down and find something else to worry about. Then you can quietly climb into your stand. Once again do not knock it until you have tried it. You will be surprised!!!

Do Not Bother the Does

One aspect of trophy hunting that many hunters do not pay attention to is the local doe herd. One of the most important things to low profile hunting for monster bucks is the fact that you should never bother the does or let the does know you are hunting. There is a time and place to thin the doe herd, but while you are trophy hunting it is not one of those times.

Treat each doe as if it were a monster buck that you were hunting, and do not let her know you are there. Many of these antlerless animals are button bucks that you will be hunting in the future. Never train them that you are hunting or that you are a threat.

Hiding from Other Hunters

Low profile hunting also means hiding from other hunters. If other hunters are walking around your stands when you are not there, it will destroy that spot for hunting. These hunters may likewise be using your stand, or think this is a great spot, and set up right next to you. You may end up wasting a few hunts at this stand before you realize that someone else has destroyed your set up.

The better you hide your stands so that other hunters do not find them, the better they will hide you when you are hunting trophy whitetails. Many of the fixed position stands which do not have chains have large black straps that hold them to the tree. These straps can be seen in the woods from hundreds of yards away. You will find if you take a roll of camouflage tape, and wrap it around the tree covering your black strap, your stand will disappear into the background. Just try this once and you will see the difference. The first tree stand manufacturer that puts camouflage straps on their stands wins!!

Ground Blinds

Many hunters do not feel comfortable in a tree or physically cannot climb into one. These hunters are restricted to hunting from the ground.

Ground blinds make great stands for long-range weapons. They are a little harder to hunt trophy bucks from with a bow. One of the good things about this type of stand is that it hides most movements of the hunter. Heavier material blinds also provide good scent control when it is cold. This is due to the fact that you warm the air inside of the blind from your body temperature. Then as the air escapes from the blind it rises. This is due to the fact that this air is warmer than the outside air, carrying your scent up and away.

Hopefully this chapter has your mind working overtime, and you frequently refer back to this chapter as you read the rest of the tactics in this book. Just remember, it is all about the odds, odds, and more odds!!!

Another great day in the field.

Chapter 7

Clothing and Equipment

Now that you have an understanding of low profile hunting in highly pressured areas, there must be an understanding of the equipment you need to be successful. In this chapter you will be presented with some options on equipment that works well. You may already have chosen good equipment to use that you have confidence in. Use this chapter as a guide to filling the voids you have in equipment selection. This will allow you to remain undetected while you are hunting that trophy of a lifetime.

K. I. S. S. System

Keep It Simple Stupid is the basis on which all of your equipment should be selected. Anytime your equipment becomes complicated there is a greater chance of failure. Choose quality gear, that is user friendly, and your odds will improve. Then you will have a better chance of being successful.

Warm Weather Gear

Many times the early part of the hunting season seems to be too hot for our comfort. It is hard not to sweat, and to keep our odor down. Luckily there are new lightweight scent-control outfits on the market. Purchase one that has a camouflage pattern, and you can wear this alone as your hunting garment.

Keep it simple and your trophy hunting odds will increase.

If biting insects are a problem early, make sure you purchase a good quality bug suit. These suits are lightweight, and allow you to sit still while those pesky bugs are flying around you trying to get in. This is important, as you know that one of the deer's key defenses is its ability to detect movement. Many of these bug suits also come in camouflage. If the scent-control garment you have on is not camouflage, these bug suits make a great warm weather outer garment.

Bear in mind that, even though it is warm out, you still must cover your hands and face. Light colored skin shows up through the cover like a neon sign to the deer, and every little movement you make is magnified by it. You move your hands and head more than any other part of your body while on stand. Why would you want to bring attention to your location by not covering these parts of your body?

Undergarments

As the weather cools down throughout the season, you will find the need for undergarments to keep yourself warm. The best way to keep warm is by layering your clothes so that you trap warm air between the garments. There are quite a few different types and materials for undergarments on the market. The better ones all work under the same concept. They wick moisture away from the body and trap warm air between the fibers of the material. Just remember to make sure you wear your scent control clothing over your undergarments and under your outer garments. Here are a couple examples of bad and good undergarments.

Cotton is probably the worst material for an undergarment to keep you warm. Cotton holds a great deal of moisture, which will cool down your body temperature. It moreover has very little ability to hold warm air. You should never wear cotton next to your skin, if you want to keep warm.

Most trophy hunters wear undergarments made of polypropylene or a material spun from synthetic fiber. These garments come in various weights for different temperatures. You will find these garments do a great job of wicking the moisture away from your skin as you sweat and have a loft that holds warm air well. By layering these types of garments, you will be able to stay in your stand for many hours in frigid weather. The longer you can stay on stand, the better your odds of taking home that trophy of a lifetime.

Outer Garments

Without talking about specific camouflage patterns, there are tons of different hunting clothes manufacturers. Even though there are so many choices, you still need guidelines on how to choose the correct outer garment for hunting.

First, determine if the garment fits properly. It must be loose enough to layer clothes under without being too tight. At the same time, it must not be too bulky. If it is overly bulky or is cut the wrong way, it could interfere with your ability to shoot your weapon.

Secondly, the garment you choose must keep you warm and protected from the elements. The better your garments perform at this, the more comfortable and longer you will be able to stay on stand.

Cotton is a poor choice due to fact that it does not retain warmth well. Likewise, cotton absorbs water easily, therefore, chilling your body quickly.

Many outdoorsmen swear that wool is the best outdoor clothing to wear. High quality wool garments are very expensive. The so-called selling feature of wool is that it retains warmth well, and it is thought that you can keep warm in wool even when it is wet. The more expensive brands of wool are very wind proof and hold warmth very well. The problem is that wool does hold water, and gets very heavy when wet. It furthermore takes a very long time to dry out. Also, there is really no proof that it does keep you warm when wet.

Polar Fleece is a synthetic fiber material. It is spun with high loft so that it retains warmth well. Fleece holds very little water and dries out in minutes. It takes a lot of rain before you get wet in fleece. You will find that it will have to

Clothing and Equipment 117

Proper clothing will keep you on stand long enough to be successful.

rain hard and long before you need to put on your rainwear if you wear fleece clothing. Also, it is very light and comfortable to wear. Most true trophy hunters use fleece as their primary clothing choice. The only downfall to fleece is that it is not extremely wind proof. You may want to purchase fleece clothing with a wind barrier. As well, fleece has a tendency to pick up seeds and burrs.

Finally, but very important, is how quiet your outer garments tend to be. Deer have great hearing, and seem to pick up the slightest noise you make when you are in your stand. More importantly is your ability to hear the deer approaching. If all you hear is the noise of your clothing every time you turn your head or move in your stand, you have diminished your odds of taking home a trophy buck.

Cotton and nylon are very noisy, especially when it is cold out. Wool and fleece on the other hand are whisper quiet. When you add up all of the various types of garments, wool is a good choice, but fleece seems to be the best choice. If you are in need of some new hunting clothes, it would be wise to buy a good fleece outfit, and then your odds will improve as you hunt this season.

Hands, Head and Face

As you read in the last chapter, you should use scent-control clothing on your head and cover your nose and mouth. This is good not only for scent control, but to camouflage the movement of your head as well. Use a hat with a small bill on it to shade and cover your eyes. Get a warm weather hat and a cold weather hat. Do not wear these hats when you are not in the field, so that they do not pick up odors.

Cover your mouth and nose with a scent-control neck gaiter. For cold weather you can get them in fleece so that they are silent. You should try to put together a system that does not cover your ears if you rely on them heavily. Make sure if you wear a face mask that it does not interfere with your ability to shoot your weapon.

Some hunters use face paint and this works well to dull the color of your face. Many grow a beard at this time of year, which also works well.

You should additionally cover your hands. Most trophy hunters use a light glove for shooting and then put their hands in their pockets or a hand muff to keep them warm. Another way to keep your hands warm is the air activated chemical warmer packs that you can buy at the sporting goods stores. These work great for hours of warmth. You can put them in your pockets or in your muff. Likewise, they work great on other parts of your body that get cold.

Just consider that, if you are not covering your head and hands, you are not being a complete low profile hunter. You have just lowered you odds on taking home that giant whitetail.

Shoes and Boots

It cannot be stressed enough how important knee high, rubber boots are for the trophy whitetail hunter. As you have learned in the previous chapter, these boots are a vital part of our low profile hunting system. These boots come in uninsulated and insulated models. If you purchase a pair of insulated boots, there is no need to buy a pair with more than 1200 grams of insulation in them. This is due to the fact that all of the insulation is on the top of the foot and only a small portion is on the sole. This is where most of the cold creeps in.

You may find out that these boots keep your feet warmer than you think. This is due to the fact that the insulation is sandwiched between two layers of rubber and does not get wet from the outside or the inside as you sweat. You should purchase a pair that fits well with only one good pair of socks. You will find them more comfortable this way, especially if you walk a long way to your stands.

Most pac style boots do not work as well due to the fact that once the lining gets wet your feet will get cold. These boots are also hard to walk any distance in. These boots furthermore retain and release a lot of human scent.

It was only four degrees the morning this buck was taken.

One alternative that works well for extreme cold weather is a military boot called the Mickey Mouse boot. They are all rubber inside and out with excellent insulation sandwiched between the rubber layers. They are very scent proof. Also, they keep warm air between the layers like an air bladder with a valve on the ankle. Make sure you purchase the true military version, as there are many cheap imitations on the market. You can find these boots at most military surplus stores

There is one more fantastic alternative to keeping your feet warm.

Boot Blankets

Do not laugh at these, as whoever invented them came up with a great way to keep your feet warm while on stand. There are two types that stand out in this type of footwear.

A company called Icebreaker makes the first type, which has been around for a long time. They are called Insulated Boot Blanket Overboots. You can walk to your stand in your knee-high rubber boots and then slip these on. Your feet will stay warm in the coldest temperatures. The only problem is that they are quite bulky to wear in a treestand.

One trick used in Canada on rifle hunts is to take off your walking boots and then put on a couple pairs of warm socks. Then slip your feet into the boot blankets with a couple of chemical hand warmers. Nothing will keep your feet warmer.

The second type of this footwear is called Boot Insulators and is made by a company called ArcticShield. They use a heat reflective material and are not as bulky as boot blankets. You can roll up a pair of these and they will fit in your coat pocket. These little boot insulators seem to work almost as well as the bulky boot blankets while taking up much less room in your pack. Both types of boot outerwear can be found at better sporting goods stores.

With the proper clothing and equipment the end of the trail can look like this.

Packs

Just like with your clothing you should carry a backpack or fanny pack made of a quiet material. There are many styles of packs made out of fleece or saddlecloth, which is very waterproof. No true trophy hunter goes into the woods without his favorite pack.

You should carry a pack that has multiple compartments to separate your gear. Then each item is easy to find even in the dark. Also, your pack should be large enough to carry everything you need for a days hunt.

Keep everything in one pack instead of constantly sticking items in your pockets. Store this pack in a scent-free container or bag. When you are ready to hunt all that you have to do is grab your pack, and your weapon, and you are ready to go.

Binoculars

Many hunters, especially bow hunters, do not feel they need to take binoculars into the field. They are wrong. A good quality, mid-priced pair of binoculars can tell a hunter many things.

While driving down the road, you should always keep a pair of binoculars by your side. You might just see, pull over, and then get a better look at a monster buck disappearing into the timber. This could lead you to a new honey hole.

While walking to or from your stand during daylight hours, you can glass the fields for a better look. Then you will know if it is all clear to proceed without alerting any deer.

When you are sitting in your stand hunting, you may see animals traveling in the thick cover. Binoculars may help you identify if any of those animals is a trophy buck worth hunting. If you do see a large buck or a couple different shooter bucks traveling the same path more than once, you should immediately plan on moving your stand to the new hot spot that you just found.

Scouting binoculars can help you locate rubs, scrapes and trails from a distance without the need to disturb the area. Finally after you have a monster whitetail down, a good pair of binoculars can help in locating him. You will be able to identify a patch of hair or an antler tine from a distance.

Flashlights and Headlamps

Never travel in the woods in the dark without a good flashlight. Also make sure you have a spare in your pack just in case. Many hunters like to walk to their stands in total darkness. This is wrong, as you tend to get off the trail to your stand leaving behind scent that could destroy your hunt.

Deer do not seem to pay attention to lights in the woods. If you walk with a light on, you will be able to follow your trail of bright eyes right to your stand. Further, you will be able to get to your stand much quicker and much quieter than you would if you were stumbling around in the dark.

Today there are many lightweight headlamps on the market. Many are very small consisting of bright LED lamps. These little beauties allow hands free travel through the woods in the dark. Also, you can easily climb into your stand with one of these lights on. Try one of these lights once and you will never be without one.

Safety Belts

This is just one more reminder to wear your safety belt or harness at all times while you are in a tree. Buy a good quality harness. There are new style vests that have safety harnesses built right into them for ease of putting on. Keep in mind that a trophy buck is not worth your life.

Mark was properly prepared when this buck came by.

Pack Accessories

Here is a list of a few other items that you should always carry in your pack. Your list may differ due to your own needs:
- Hunting license
- Skinning knife
- Extra rope (30 feet)
- Bright eyes
- Water bottle
- Urine bottle
- Extra gloves
- Spare release
- Lunch
- Flashlight
- Hand pruner
- Hand saw
- Spare batteries
- Compass or GPS unit
- Extra hand warmers
- Extra tree steps

Treestand Accessories

There are a few items that can make your hunt worthwhile and sitting in a tree more enjoyable.

Always have a bow or gun rope hanging from your existing stands. Then you will not have to put your weapon on the ground.

If you hunt with a bow and like to take your quiver off, purchase a screw-in quiver holder. You will find these at any good sporting goods stores. Quiver holders allow you to keep your arrows out of the way but just within reach right where you want them. These holders allow you to pull out an arrow very quietly. Likewise, you do not have to worry about knocking your quiver to the ground.

Go to the home improvement store and purchase a couple of screw in broom holders. These little, two-pronged hooks work great for hanging your bow, gun, pack, or any

Clothing and Equipment **127**

Having an ATV is another great piece of equipment.

other items in your tree. They screw in easier than the bow hooks that you can buy at the sporting goods store. Also, they usually are dipped in brightly coated rubber. This makes them easier to find in the dark, or if you drop one to the ground.

Likewise, many sporting goods stores sell screw in arms of various lengths. These are great for keeping your bow in just the right spot and allowing you hunt without holding your weapon in your hands constantly.

Light vs. Dark Camouflage

Finally you should know the difference in camouflage patterns. It really does not matter what brand of camouflage you wear. The important thing is how light the pattern is.

The darker the pattern on your clothes, the more you look like a giant dark blob at a distance. The lighter your camouflage clothes are, the better you will blend in to your background.

Take this test. Stand outside in the sunlight. Pick up any plate sized object and look at it from above. Then raise your hand above your head and look at it from below. You will not believe how much darker the object is when you look at it from below. This is due to the shade on the underside of the object. This is how a deer sees you in your stand. The shadows make your clothing look much darker than the true color of your camouflage.

One simple trick is to take a very dark pattern and a very light pattern, and hang them in the woods at a distance. You will immediately see a big difference, and you will forever think differently about camouflage clothes and their patterns.

Chapter 8

Weapons of Choice

In this chapter we will discuss the choice of weapons that are available to take into the field. Always recognize that the choice you make will help determine the odds of harvesting that trophy whitetail when he presents himself.

There are thousands of choices when it comes to hunting weapons. Many of these weapons, in various combinations, will perform well. To get in depth on each weapon would take a book in itself. This chapter will give just an overview of the best choices for each hunting season.

The first thing you must understand is that, if you do not hunt every available season for each weapon, you will greatly reduce your odds of taking home that monster buck. If you are primarily a bowhunter, you should not skip gun season or muzzleloader season. To do so would cut your odds in half.

The second thing to keep in mind is not to take a knife to a gunfight, as the old adage states. Do not bow hunt during the gun season, unless the area you are hunting is bowhunting only. There is nothing worse than having the buck of your lifetime standing at sixty yards and you can do nothing about it. It will be hard to forgive yourself, just because you decided to hunt with your bow.

Your mind is your most important weapon.

Your Mind

Your mind is your most important weapon you own. The most important thing to your success will be by thinking and making the right choices at the right time. Your quarry is very competent at survival, and it is your mind that usually tips the odds in your favor over anything else that you possess.

All of your preplanning and scouting earlier in the year will put that monster buck in front of you. Using the right weapon and taking him home is just a quick culmination to all of your hard work.

Bows and Arrows

The proper weapon when it comes to bows and arrows is very controversial. Please remember that we are discussing the proper weapons for hunting large mature whitetails.

The craze today is for hunters to use traditional equipment consisting of recurve bows and longbows. The truth is that probably only ten percent of the traditional hunters can finalize the deal at the moment of truth on a mature whitetail buck. The ten percent that can make this happen are great hunters. They use heavy enough equipment, and have the shooting skills that rival modern archery equipment. These hunters understand that a trophy buck has a much larger body and bone structure than a year and a half old animal. They realize that when they are trophy hunting it is not the place for forty-pound bows and lightweight arrows.

For the vast majority of hunters, the modern compound bow is a much better choice when chasing that buck of their dreams. This equipment is capable of more consistent shot placement under stress for most hunters.

There are many options when it comes to modern compound bows. It is mostly personal choice of the hunter what brand or model to shoot. There are only a couple of things to consider when setting up your equipment for trophy whitetail hunting.

Make sure your bow can handle large bodied mature bucks.

The first thing you should use is the K.I.S.S. system that we talked about earlier in this book. Typically the simpler that you keep your bow set up, the more consistently it performs. The more complicated your set up is or the more moving parts that you have will lend itself to a better chance of failure at the moment of truth when the shot occurs.

No matter what bow you decide to hunt with it must be capable of shooting completely through a three hundred pound deer. If you look at almost any successful big buck hunter's set up, you will see that their equipment is capable of shooting through a large buck at any angle. This is very important, as you will get very few chances at a mature animal. You will further find it is very rare that a mature buck will give you a perfect broadside shot.

Many outdoorsmen feel that the only ethical shot is a broadside or quartering away shot. This is the preferred shot on game, but rarely happens in the field on mature whitetails. As a mature buck approaches your stand, it is very hard to get him to walk past your stand without thinking something is wrong. Normally you will have to take the first decent opportunity that is available to you. If you do not, your odds drastically drop from that point on that you will get another shot opportunity. This usually means that you might have to take a shot that is not from the "preferred" angle.

A mature buck's vital area is about the size of a basketball. If you have the equipment capable of completely shooting through this basketball from any angle, the shot should not be considered unethical. This does not mean you should over bow yourself with a heavy draw weight that makes shooting accurately difficult. There are many set ups in the sixty-pound range that are excellent for having the penetration you need.

These past statements might raise a few hairs on a few sportsmen's necks, but any true trophy hunter understands the importance in being able to harvest a giant buck from any angle if necessary. This book was not written to tell you only what you wanted to hear, but was written to tell you the truth, and to help you make the dream of taking home monster bucks a reality.

There are only a few things to be aware of when setting up your bow. Your odds normally go up when you use some sort of sight system verses shooting instinctively. This system should be strong and simple with few moving parts. It should have a second point of reference such as a peep for better accuracy.

Also, there is much controversy over using aluminum arrows verses carbon arrows. The truth is they both work great as long as they have the correct spine for your bow set up. The thing to consider here is that most successful trophy hunters lean towards heavy arrows for increased penetration.

Finally one of the biggest questions is whether to use fixed bladed broadheads or mechanical broadheads. You will find most big buck hunters rely on fixed heads. Mechanical heads usually have poor penetration on bone. Likewise, they have a tendency to deflect off animals when shot at an extreme angle. In addition, they have moving parts that provide for the possibility of failure.

Shotguns

Many highly populated states only allow shotguns during gun season. Today's shotgun is a great hunting weapon. If you truly want to chase giant whitetails and are primarily a bowhunter, do not pass up this season if you want to better your odds at taking home those trophy bucks.

There are two types of shotguns to consider. The first is a gun to use while sitting on stand. There are many guns capable of shooting slugs accurately out to one hundred seventy five yards or better. These are usually single shot or bolt-action guns. Combine the rifled barrel of these guns with a good three to nine power scope and you can reach out and touch some game.

The second type of gun to consider is a rifle barreled pump or semi-automatic slug gun with trueglow fixed sights. This is considered a brush gun. This type of gun is

Here is a great shotgun buck.

great when making deer drives. It allows for quick sighting on game combined with excellent shooting.

Rifles

Most highly pressured areas do not permit rifles during the gun season. If you do live in one of the lucky states that allow rifles like Kentucky, most of the traditional cartridges will work fine when trophy hunting. Just remember to set up one gun for a stand gun and one gun for a brush gun, just like with shotguns. You will notice most well-known trophy hunters use cartridges between .270 and .300. This way they have enough energy to take down a large whitetail.

Muzzleloaders

Many states now have a special season for muzzleloaders, often called a primitive weapons' season. You should take advantage of this season, if you want to improve your odds on trophy bucks. Many of these guns can shoot well out to two hundred yards.

The newer in-line muzzleloaders are more reliable than the old percussion models. Therefore, you should consider an in-line model when you purchase one. Make sure you mount a good scope on your gun, if your state allows it. Most of the newer guns are simple to load and clean making them a great weapon to chase those big bucks.

Handguns

Some states allow handguns during gun season. There really is no use for handguns in trophy hunting when there are better options to use during gun season. To use one would only be personal preference. Presently there are no special handgun seasons that would make this a good choice of weapon. The only real reason to use one would be if you were trying to break a handgun record.

This buck was taken with a muzzleloader.

Crossbows

The crossbow is a weapon surrounded by much controversy. This weapon is great for handicap bowhunters, but do not disregard the crossbow when trophy hunting. Presently more and more states are allowing crossbow hunting during the archery season. There are a couple of situations when the crossbow shines.

The first situation is during late archery season when there is little cover to hide your movements. When there is a large group of deer around you and a trophy buck shows up, it is hard to draw a conventional bow without drawing a lot of attention. Highly pressured whitetails do not let you get away with much, as they are extremely wary. With a crossbow all you have to do is aim and pull the trigger.

The second situation is one that only a few smart trophy deer hunters are taking advantage of when it presents itself. Many sanctuaries, where large bucks die of old age, are surrounded by nothing but open fields. Most hunters will not ask for permission to hunt such places due to the lack of cover. Since hunters rarely bother these landowners, many times it is easy to gain permission to hunt.

Once you gain permission, it is easy to set up by lying prone on the ground and covering yourself in corn stalks, grass, camouflage cloth, or snow camouflage. When the deer come out to feed in the evening all you have to do is pull the trigger on that monster buck!

This one trick could double the amount of trophy buck property that you have permission to hunt. I bet your brain is working overtime on that one!!

Chapter 9

Scents, Calling, Decoys and Baiting

This chapter might just be the most controversial chapter ever written in a deer hunting book. You can probably hear the deer hunting community grumbling and freaking out as you read this. You told yourself you wanted to know the truth about trophy buck hunting in highly pressured areas. That is why you bought this book.

You are about to read three very harsh statements. After your head stops reeling from reading these few statements, you can continue to read this chapter. If you can accept what you learn from this point forward, you will be on your way to consistently being within range of those monster bucks you dream about!

Statement #1:
If you want to consistently take trophy whitetails in a highly pressured area or any area for that matter, you should be willing to use any legal method available!!!

Statement #2:
None of the trophy whitetail bucks pictured in this book have been taken with the use of calls, rattling horns, scents or decoys, or have been taken over scrapes or rub-lines!!!

Statement #3:
Contrary to normal beliefs, in states where it is legal and especially in states where they have a late archery season, a large percentage of mature bucks are taken over bait!!!

Holy cow!!! Go back and read that again! You know you can't wait to tell your hunting buddies what you just read in a deer hunting book! Good!! Everyone should learn the truth!!

First, please realize that this book is not criticizing scents, calling, rattling, and decoying. These tactics may work great in areas of low hunting pressure, especially west of the Mississippi River. With this in mind, their uses are minimal in highly pressured hunting environments where most of the deer hunting population hunts. Each tactic will be explained further in this chapter.

Secondly, this book is not a book about baiting. The majority of the bucks pictured in this book were not taken over bait. Bait did play a factor in a few of these deer and will be discussed at the end of this chapter as one of the tactics you should use as a trophy deer hunter.

Next, hunting near scrapes and rub-lines are great strategies in areas with low hunting pressure, a good buck age structure, and a close doe-to-buck ratio. The problem is that the rest of us hunt in the real world. This is a world where the woods are full of hunters. Furthermore, this is a world where the majority of the surviving bucks are only one and a half years old, and there are forty does to every buck. Under these conditions, rubs and scrapes play a very minor role in our trophy hunting strategies that will be covered in the following chapters.

Finally, realize there are exceptions to every rule, but they are few and far between.

Scents

The first thing you must bear in mind, as we discuss the various deer attractors like scents, is the whole premise of this book is about low profile hunting and not letting the deer know you exist. Always remember that no scent is usually the best scent. When you apply scent trails or place scent canisters around your stand, you are leaving human scent behind at the same time. There are four basic types of scents that a hunter can use.

The first type of scent is a food attractant scent like apple or acorn scent. This type of scent normally has no place in a trophy hunting strategy.

The second type of scent many hunters use is cover scents like fox urine, raccoon urine or skunk scent. Skunk scent is normally considered a sign of danger to most animals. Deer normally do not have a favorable reaction to these scents and usually will not tolerate them, especially mature bucks.

The third and latest fad in scents is a dominant buck scent. This scent is supposed to attract other bucks by fooling them into thinking another buck has entered their territory. In most highly pressured areas the buck age structure is a mess and there are dozens of does for every breeding buck. There is no reason for a mature buck to look for conflict with another buck under these conditions.

The final type of scent is a doe in estrus scent. You may find that this scent has a use in your trophy hunting strategy. Of all, the deer attractant scents are the least used compared to calls and rattling horns. This is due to the fact that scents are quite expensive and do not last year to year like the other attractants. This means the deer are less likely to have come in contact with another hunter using scents.

You should only use doe estrus scent during two very short time frames of the season. The mature bucks know when the does should be coming into heat and will not respond in a positive manner, if you use this scent at the wrong time.

The first period is during the four or five days just before the first doe comes into heat. This is considered the pre-rut period known as the trolling phase or chasing and seeking phase.

The second time frame is the four or five days after the last doe has been bred or came out of heat. This is known as the post-rut period.

The place that estrus scent seems to work best is when you are hunting next to some type of sanctuary such as a metropark where the mature bucks have never come in contact with a hunter using scents. It is even better if it is legal to walk onto the sanctuary as long as you are not hunting.

If it is legal in your state, the best method is to walk with a scent drag and make a large circle or oval in the sanctuary from your stand and then back to your stand again. Any mature buck that comes into contact with the scent trail should follow it back to your stand no matter which way he follows the trail. If you can travel two directions from your stand you can make a scent trail in the form of a large figure eight with your stand at the apex of the two circles. This is a great way to pull giant bucks out of a sanctuary onto your hunting spot, especially if there is no other reason for them to come by your stand.

If you do decide to use this little trick, it is best if you lay your scent trail right after daylight so you can see where you are going. Then after the bucks get up around 9:00 in the morning and start trolling looking for hot does you could be in for some great action. Remember to sit all day on this stand because a trophy buck could come by at any time.

Always keep in mind to only do this when the wind is in your favor. Likewise, be careful of leaving any human scent behind when making a scent trail. The only major downfall to this trick is that the bucks may come to your set up after you leave in the evening. Once fooled by this trick, they will be hard to fool again.

There goes that mind of yours again!! Now you are thinking of all the places this might work!!!

Calling

Nowadays it seem like every tree in the woods has someone in it grunting or bleating with a deer call. Every deer in the woods in a highly pressured area relates this calling to a hunter. If you want to keep a low profile while hunting, it is better to leave your calls at home.

Scents, Calling, Decoys and Baiting 143

This is the view from one of my best stands where normal tactics you read about do not work.

Many experts claim that they have never had a negative reaction to a call. This should not be considered true. If a buck acts like he never heard your call but slinks away through the woods never to be seen again, it is a negative reaction. Many bucks hear your calling and then wait until after you leave your stand to investigate the area. If they pick up that you were hunting them and avoid this area, this is a negative reaction. Finally, if a mature buck comes to your call but circles downwind and locates you, then left without your getting a shot, it is also a negative reaction. Your chance of ever getting a shot at this buck again is very slim.

In recent years it seems that the deer herd has learned not to be so vocal. They seem to relate this to danger. Just like they have evolved to looking into trees for danger, they have decided not to vocalize much. Rarely do you hear the bucks grunting as they chase does anymore. In the old days when a deer smelled you or caught sight of you they would give a loud warning snort. Today they usually just slink away without a sound. When was the last time you heard a deer snort in the woods?

Bear in mind once again, when hunting highly pressured whitetails on small parcels of land, you should leave your calls at home. You should not help bucks locate your stand and train them to avoid your set up with calling.

Rattling

Rattling is in the same category as calling. In most pressured areas you can hear someone using rattling horns in every woodlot. If you use this method in highly pressured areas, nine times out of ten you will just be teaching the deer herd where your stand is.

You should additionally recognize that mature bucks in these highly pressured areas do not need to compete for does. There is no reason for them to want to fight another buck. To rattle under these conditions should be considered a mistake.

Scents, Calling, Decoys and Baiting 145

**The only horns I carry in the woods
are the ones I find and pick up.**

Decoys

Decoys provide for a very entertaining way to hunt. They bring with them a large amount of deer activity and action. They do have a few downfalls though.

First, most decoys are very awkward and noisy to carry and set up in the woods. Their noise and weight makes it difficult to keep a low profile while hunting.

Secondly, if a decoy has duped a buck once and you do not take him, the chances of them coming in again are rare.

Next, small bucks in an unbalanced herd will destroy your set up usually long before a mature buck shows up. These small bucks have a tendency to knock your decoy over or become alarmed and warn the rest of the herd.

Finally, if your decoy is visible from a distance other hunters will destroy your hunt and locate your stand by stalking this fake deer.

Baiting

Baiting is probably the most controversial subject in hunting circles. There have been many articles written on the pros and cons of baiting. Most hunters believe that mature bucks cannot be brought in by bait. Many hunters feel that baiting is only a last resort for rookie hunters looking to take home a doe. They are all wrong!!!

The truth is that a large majority of the monster bucks shot in Canada are taken over bait. Think about this. If you spent big money to go trophy whitetail hunting in Canada, and it is legal to use bait in the providence you are hunting, you will probably find that you spend most of your time hunting over bait. There are a few exceptions with some outfitters.

The reason bait is used in Canada is that there are very few deer in most areas. Baiting draws these animals to one small area. Food is hard to come by in these harsh conditions. The bait brings in the does who in turn draw in the bucks.

Texas is another fine example of the use of bait for trophy bucks. As you sit in a tripod stand looking down cut-lines through the bush called senderos spreading out from your stand like spokes on a wagon wheel, you are looking at one big bait pile as trucks with corn filled spreaders drop bait down each one. This is done due to the brush being so thick you need a reason for the deer to step into the open. When the does come out to feed in the open the bucks soon follow.

While you watch a big name hunter on TV telling you he is hunting an "acorn" patch, what he really means is a corn patch! You need to open your eyes. You have been watching hunting shows in Canada and Texas on TV for years wishing that you were there.

If you want to be consistent on taking trophy bucks, and it is legal in your state, you need to add baiting to your hunting bag of tricks. If the word "baiting" offends you, consider calling it the more politically correct term "supplemental feeding."

With all those articles out there on baiting, very few tell you the correct way to do it. For your information, the hunters out there that consistently take monster bucks over bait are professionals, and they have the system down to a science. There is no reason you shouldn't do the same.

There are two times during the season that baiting works best. The first is during the periods of pre-rut, rut and post-rut. The second is during the late season.

The preferred type of feed is usually apples or shelled corn sometimes used in conjunction with molasses. The use of molasses is due to its strong aromatic smell and ability to draw deer from a great distance.

There are two choices where to place your stand when using bait. You can hunt directly over the bait or place your stand in a funnel between the bait and a bedding area, if you prefer.

Here are a couple thoughts on stand placement. When you use bait you have total control of where the deer come to. This usually works best when you are hunting a small parcel of property next to some type of sanctuary. Especially when the deer normally have no reason to pass through this property. Make sure you pick a tree with plenty of cover for a stand site. Do not worry about existing deer trails. Pick a tree where the wind is normally in your favor and the deer cannot get downwind of you easily. Make sure you can get to your stand unseen and unheard by the deer.

During the three stages of the rut, it is usually better to sit directly over the bait due to the fact a mature buck can show up from any direction. You should plan on sitting on stand all day. The reason these bucks are showing up is not because they are hungry, but because they are looking for hot does. If he is with a doe at the time, he may follow her right in. At this time of year, you should be set up in fairly thick cover where the bucks will feel comfortable coming to you in the middle of the day. If possible, put down plenty of feed so you do not disturb the deer often and the deer do not run out of food and go somewhere else. It is usually best if you crib the far side of your set up with a pile of branches or a large tree trunk. This will keep the deer from facing you head on. The deer will be forced to stand broadside or quartering away for much better shot placement.

During the late season when food is a priority it is better to set up in an area with less cover. You do not want the deer to feed all day at your set up. You want to be in cover just thick enough the deer will feel comfortable to come out to feed before the end of hunting hours. If it is too open, they will wait until after dark. You should only hunt in the afternoon until dark at this time of year. The deer are usually herded up in these sanctuaries at this time of year and come out in droves to feed in the evening. Due to this fact, it is a good time to hunt funnels between bedding areas and the food source. This way you may take a mature buck coming in at the last moment. Furthermore, you have the ability to leave your stand without alarming all of the deer at your bait station.

There is one trick that can help during this time of year. Unlike earlier in the year when you want a large amount of food on the ground, at this time of year you want just enough food out to make the deer compete for it every evening. As soon as they learn that it is first-come, first-serve before the food runs out, they will come out earlier than normal. Those big bucks want their share as much as everyone else.

Chapter 10

The Early Season

Can you believe that you read nine chapters before we discussed what to do during the hunting season? This is due to the fact that hunting mature whitetail bucks is ninety percent preparation and only ten percent sitting on a stand.

In a few states deer hunting season starts in mid September, but the majority of states start their archery deer season in early October. If your season starts early enough you may be able to catch bucks still in their bachelor groups.

Glassing

If you like to watch fields in September with a spotting scope, try to hold off until approximately one week before season due to constant changing of the behavior of mature bucks this time of year. You will pressure these bucks off your fields, if you watch them too much. You should consider the first couple days of the season one of the best times of the year to harvest a mature buck, only surpassed by the rut and then the late season.

Mornings

One of the biggest mistakes hunters make is locating a giant buck feeding in a field and then on opening day hunting that area in the morning! What are they thinking?

Never try to hunt mornings on opening day unless you have a stand where you can catch the buck returning to his bedding area. Make sure you do not have to cross open fields to get to your stand. If a big buck sees you coming across the fields in the morning, he will not be coming out to those same fields to feed in the evening until after dark. By hunting only evenings in early October, your success rate should increase greatly.

Speed Scouting

If you know there are mature bucks in your area but have not had the time to watch for them, or your ground is too hilly to watch from a great distance, this is a strategy you might find most effective. Wait until early afternoon on opening day. Then carry a stand to the edge of the field you feel the bucks are feeding in. Enter the woods about thirty yards from the edge of the field and walk the perimeter looking for large rubs and tracks on trails heading to the field. On trails where bucks enter the field, the rubs will be facing away from the field. When you find a trail that you think has the most tracks and rubs, set your stand downwind of this trail about another twenty yards farther back in the woods. This is so the bucks will not smell where you've walked. Hunt that stand that evening. The deer will not know you were ever there before today. This will not always work, but it will sure up your odds. You should do this in different areas each evening for the first few days of the season. This should guarantee that each stand is fresh that day.

Water

If you experience hot/dry fall weather, water will be a priority to a deer. A mature buck usually will go to a water source every evening before going to feed. You can catch him going between his bedding area and a water source if you are careful. It does not take much of a water hole to make a deer happy. This could be a small ditch that holds

The Early Season 151

An early season buck taken near water.

water or just a puddle in the ground. The less water available, the better your chances will be to have a monster buck show up.

If you do not have water on or close to your hunting property, you will not hold deer. You should fix this by creating your own water source. You can do this in many ways. You can dig a small pond or just a hole in the ground that holds water.

One trick that you can use is to dig a hole and install a small plastic children's pool in the ground. You can place these in small pockets of cover where a buck will feel comfortable coming to before nightfall. Then all you have to do is keep it filled with water. If it is too hard to truck water to your secret spot, you can install a simple point well next to your water hole. This works great in those small woodlots out in the middle of nowhere.

Stay Out

Please read this section carefully. The best hunting strategy you can use after the first couple of days in October is to stay out of the woods and leave your properties alone!! Read the last statement again. Trophy buck hunting is all about timing.

After all the hunters hit the woods in your highly pressured area, the mature bucks will become completely nocturnal. You will not see any predictable daytime buck movement until the pre-rut in early November.

As all the other hunters put pressure on your county the mature bucks will slowly relocate to where they feel safe and there is no hunting pressure. These animals end up in all of the sanctuaries we discussed earlier in this book.

The trick is to make your properties feel like sanctuaries to these animals. If they find no hunting pressure on your property they will feel as safe as if they were in a park. This trick can bring you big bucks from miles and stack them up on your property. If your property is connected to an already existing sanctuary, the deer will feel that your property is just an extension of their already safe zone.

A late October cold front had this buck on the move.

The good news is at the end of October you will be able to use all of the low profile hunting strategies that you have learned so far. When pre-rut begins, those monster bucks will feel safe traveling during daylight hours and then you can capitalize on the best hunting of the season. How to do this will be covered in the next chapter.

Mid-October

If you have ants in your pants and just cannot stay out of the woods here are a few suggestions.

If you must sit in a tree at this time of year, try to go only when a cold front occurs. The bucks do not move much during hot weather and the cool air that comes with a front sometimes puts them on the move.

If you have permission on multiple properties you can just hunt one and leave the rest of your properties alone. This way if you put too much pressure on the property you are hunting you will have backup properties when the real action begins.

If you like venison and would like to take a few does home, this might be the time for you to do it. Hunt any area where you do not have the trophy bucks you are looking for. You should have located plenty of these type areas in the spring when you were looking for properties to hunt.

Finally, GO FISHING!! At least you are outdoors.

Corn

Many hunters do not understand the significance of standing corn and how deer relate to it. When the hunting pressure is on, big bucks in the area will use standing corn as their bedding and security cover, if it is available.

Most hunters think that deer travel from the woods to the standing corn in the evening. This is usually incorrect. A mature buck normally beds during the day within the cornfield. As evening approaches he will move toward a source of water that may be in the woods. Then after a

This buck came out of the corn in the evening and into the woods.

drink he heads towards the fields to feed or to the woods for acorns.

One little secret to keep in mind is that a large mature buck with a wide rack does not fit down cornrows very well. When hunting around cornfields, concentrate on areas that the corn is stunted and is not very tall. Bucks will be prone to travel through these areas.

Chapter 11

November

November is usually the most important month of the year for most trophy whitetail hunters. The fact is that more mature bucks are taken during the month of November than during the rest of the season combined. This is primarily due to the fact that this is the breeding time for deer called the rut. The only areas where there might be an exception are the Deep South and Texas where the rut usually occurs in December and January. The Midwest and East though consider November the magic time of year

The Rut

Mature bucks rarely move during daylight hours in areas of high hunting pressure. One of the few things that can make them take a chance and travel during daylight hours is the thought of a doe in estrus. This time period is usually from a few days before Halloween until late November.

Now that you have stayed out of your hunting areas for a few weeks, the deer should be stacked up in them including a few monster bucks. This is the time of year for you to spend as much time in the woods as you can. If you have saved your vacation for hunting, this is the time for you to burn it.

Many hunters spend their time hunting over scrapes with poor success.

Different Phases of the Rut

There are many books and articles defining every little nuance of the rut. This is great information but most of it is not necessary for you to be successful at trophy whitetail hunting. The most important information you need to know in highly pressured areas is when the bucks and does are breeding and when they are not. This time of year is divided into three phases called the pre-rut, rut and post-rut.

The pre-rut is defined as the time just before the first doe enters estrus. Most hunters make a huge mistake by thinking that when they see small immature bucks chasing does around in October it is the pre-rut or sometimes even the rut itself. This activity should be ignored and not used as a gauge to define a rutting period for mature bucks.

Big, mature bucks have been around for awhile and understand that they do not have to involve themselves in chasing does until it is truly the right time. Many hunters make the mistake of shooting an immature animal because they mistake all of the chasing around as the rut. This fact has saved many a big buck's life.

Three or four days before the first doe goes into estrus the mature bucks in your area will get out of their beds and may be found traveling at any time during the day. This timing may vary by a few days between different hunting areas. At this time of year your job is to be patient until this happens and then make sure you spend as much time in the woods as possible. This is your number one chance all season to take a mature animal. You need to skip everything else and spend your time hunting during this brief period, if you want to truly have a chance at a monster buck.

Once the does go into estrus it will be much harder to locate a mature buck. This is the period known as the rut. At this time a big buck will hook up with a hot doe and spend all day in a thicket tending her. In highly pressured areas, rarely will they venture towards a feeding area before darkness falls.

In most areas with high hunting pressure, the doe-to-buck ratio is heavily weighted in the does' favor. After a

This buck was traveling between bedding areas looking for does.

mature buck spends a couple of days breeding a doe, he will take off in search of another. When there are many receptive does to pick from, he does not have to go far. This will usually occur at night under the cover of darkness. This makes it very hard to locate a shooter.

If you have not connected by now, all is not lost. After the last doe comes out of estrus there is a period called the post-rut. For a couple of days during this time the big bucks travel frantically looking for one more hot doe. At this time you may catch a shooter moving during daylight hours doing the same things that he did during the pre-rut.

This brief period will only last a couple of days before the mature bucks pick up on the fact that the rut is over. Then these animals seem to disappear as they crawl into the thickets to recover from the frantic breeding season. Other than the forced movement of gun season, your next and final chance of the season will be during late season. This is when the need for food for survival will force the bucks to move once again during daylight hours.

Cold Fronts

Impending cold fronts at this time of year will greatly improve your odds. The dropping of temperature seems to make the deer much more active. You should keep tabs on the upcoming weather and plan your hunting days around it. On these extra cool or rainy days, spend as much time in the woods as possible. This is another factor that will up your odds and may lead to that trophy of a lifetime.

Small vs. Big Woods

When hunting during the rut, one way to improve your odds is hunting the right kind of cover. In areas of heavy timber, the deer have many choices of directions to travel. It can be very hard to get a big buck within range, if his travel possibilities are unlimited.

By choosing to hunt areas with sparse cover, it limits the choices that these mature bucks can take while they

This huge buck came out of a small woodlot.

are heavily traveling looking for hot does. You must be careful though that the cover is not too sparse that it does not give these mature animals enough protection to be comfortable moving during the day. If this is the case, their survival instincts will outweigh their need to breed, and they will wait until darkness before they go on their search for a receptive doe.

Funnels

Once you find the proper type of cover that holds those big bucks, it is time to set up on them. Any pinch-point between two doe bedding areas during the pre-rut and post-rut can be phenomenal. These tight travel areas rarely have much big buck sign in them. Sometimes they will not show any signs of deer use at all. You must remain confident in the fact that, if a buck wants to travel from one doe bedding area to another in search of a hot doe, he will travel past your stand. He will do so because he wants to keep concealed, and he will feel safe in his travels.

There are dozens of books and articles about how to find and hunt funnels. Many of the best books are listed in chapter four. To describe all the types of funnels would take a book in itself. Hopefully you are already familiar with the concept before you obtained this book. If not please spend the time to research this very important strategy in your trophy whitetail hunting arsenal.

Once you become familiar with hunting funnels, you will probably make this your number one type of setup for your stands. Most good funnels will produce year after year. You must keep in mind that there is a time and place to sit in a funnel for it to be productive.

Doe Bedding Areas

Hunting the downwind side of doe bedding areas is another great strategy for this time of year. In larger timber where funnels are harder to find, this may be your

Lakes make great funnels as the deer go around them.

preferred tactic. Most bedding areas are dense thickets within the more open cover.

While bucks travel from bedding area to bedding area, they will circle the downwind side of these thickets, scent checking them for hot does. By placing your stands on these downwind edges, you will be in place to intercept them. While hunting these types of stands, consider that you must be careful not to spook the deer as you enter and exit. Once again you should only hunt these stands during the pre-rut and post-rut.

Morning vs. Evening Hunting

There is always controversy over whether mornings or evenings provide the best hunting. You will usually find evening hunts better during the early and late seasons. During the rutting phases mornings seem to be more productive. The truth of the matter is, that during November, anytime you can spend sitting on stand will up your odds in taking a mature whitetail buck.

Midday Hunting

One very important fact that many hunters overlook is that many of the largest bucks are taken during midday. Do not be afraid to sleep in and hunt during the hours of 10:00 a.m. and 2:00 p.m. during the rut. Most mature animals seem to realize that the woods are vacant of hunters during this part of the day. The need to breed will get those big bucks up on their feet and moving during these hours.

All Day Hunting

All day hunting is a very hard thing to do. If you want to be successful and are dedicated to hunting trophy whitetails, you must be prepared to sit all day on stand. During the pre-rut and post-rut periods a big buck could be on the move at anytime during the day. If you do not have any other time to hunt during the season, make sure you hunt all day during this time and your odds will skyrocket in your hunt for that trophy of a lifetime.

Scrapes and Rubs?

Although scrapes and rubs are one of the hottest topics in deer hunting circles, the truth is, they should not play a big role in your hunting strategy for monster bucks in highly pressured areas! Holy cow!! You are now thinking this sure is a bold statement that goes against everything else that you have ever read.

The truth is that this type of sign is a great indicator that a big buck is in the area. You should be encouraged when you see this sign that you are hunting the right place. Other than this fact it is usually not of much more use to you than that.

Big bucks are few and far between in highly pressured areas. These animals do not need to actively compete for does. Many of these animals leave very few rutting signs in the woods. If they do make major rubs or scrapes, it is usually in their core bedding area. These areas are very difficult to hunt without spooking the animal out of your hunting area and onto the neighbor's property.

You need to bear in mind that in areas where the deer come in constant contact with humans, cars, dogs, farming machinery, etc., they do not have consistent travel patterns. A buck may be in one area today and something may push him to another area possibly more than a mile away tomorrow. Also, they have a tendency to travel open fields at night leaving very little sign for you to pattern them.

Finally, one of the biggest reasons that much of the sign left behind may not be useful is that the buck that made the sign may be miles away on the day you are hunting. He could be traveling looking for does or possibly with a hot doe during the rut. This is why many of the best funnels to hunt have very little deer sign in them. Chew on that concept for awhile!!

We like to see big rubs but do not usually hunt next to them.

Hunting Trails?

Many hunters sit on deer trails waiting for that big buck to come by. The truth is that most of these trails were made by does early in the season when the cover was green and thick. Rarely does a mature buck use these trails.

After the leaves drop and the cover thins out in the fall, the deer gravitate to thicker cover for their travels. This is why we set all of our stands post season, when the woods are a copy of how they look in the fall. As the deer travel through this slightly thicker cover, they do not need to use trails. They have a tendency to meander back and forth as they travel in any particular direction.

Likewise, mature bucks use this slightly thicker cover for protection as they travel. This creates the funnels that you should look for. You need to have confidence in your stands placed in these areas. You need to believe that a big buck will come by even when you do not see much sign.

Leave the Does Alone

As discussed in chapter six you need to keep in mind to leave the doe herd alone. This fact is brought up again as it is very important to your trophy hunting strategy. If you need or want to kill does, do it on a property you do not plan on trophy hunting or only hunt them on one small portion of the property you are trophy whitetail hunting.

Great Stands on Multiple Properties

One great strategy to use if you have access to multiple properties is to have one or two good stands placed on each property verses having multiple stands placed on one property. This allows you to constantly rotate stands and hunt different deer each time you go out. This is one way to greatly improve your odds once again.

This strategy can save your season, especially if one or more of your hunting properties become devoid of deer due to hunting pressure or some type of other disturbance.

There is a time and place to hunt does.

Besides, some properties do not have trophy bucks on them every year.

When to Get Aggressive

The major concept of this book is low profile hunting. However, there are times that you need to get aggressive in your hunting.

If you see a big buck or multiple bucks traveling the same path more than once, you need to immediately move your stand to that location. Just because you do not understand why these animals are traveling through this location does not mean that they do not have a good reason for doing so. Do not sit back and watch these animals from afar. Make the move, and make it immediately. Do not wait until a future date to hunt this stand as it is hot today.

If you find a hot doe, do not leave to hunt another area. Put the pressure on your stands leading into the area now as a big buck could come looking for her at anytime.

Many trophy hunters say that you should never hunt the same stand more than one day in a row. This is normally good advice. The fact is that if you have a hot stand during the rut, and are seeing many bucks traveling through your set up, you do not necessarily need to abandon the stand after one sitting. If the wind is right and you can get in and out of your stand without crossing the area the bucks are traveling or disturbing any deer, you should continue to hunt this stand, if you have confidence that sooner or later a mature buck will travel through.

Bait

The process of using bait was covered in chapter nine. If you only have a small parcel of land to hunt, bait may be your only option to get a mature buck to enter your property. Once again make sure it is legal in your state. Make sure you sit on stand all day during the pre-rut and post-rut when you are using bait. A big whitetail buck can show up at anytime looking for a hot doe trail leaving the bait. Realize if you want the greatest odds of taking home a trophy buck, you need to be willing to use any legal tactic necessary.

Aggressive and Non-Aggressive Animals

Two and a half year old and three and a half year old bucks are usually fairly aggressive. They are constantly trying to compete for status in the herd. These are trophy bucks to most people in most areas. Their aggressiveness has a tendency to get them killed at this age.

Four and a half year old bucks and older seem to become very non-aggressive animals in highly pressured areas. They do not need to compete for does and usually leave very little rutting sign. These trophy animals spend all of their time working on survival. They do not tolerate mistakes by hunters. This is why low profile hunting is the best strategy to use against them. You must have confidence that these animals live in your area, and it will help you get through the season.

Big Bucks Make Noise

There are many stories on how huge monster bucks sneak through the woods and never make a sound. The fact is that a mature buck weighs much more than other younger deer in the herd. A mature animal never makes a move until he is convinced it is absolutely safe to travel. When he does move due to the fact of his size and weight, he makes a lot of noise. You usually will hear him coming from quite some distance. If the cover is heavy, you will hear the branches breaking and possibly his rack hitting tree limbs.

If a large buck does sneak into range, it is usually because it is very wet on the ground or he is walking on pine needles or soft sand. Normally they will give their location away with some noise.

This buck was heard coming from a long ways.

Typical Big Buck's Day During the Rut

The following is a typical trophy buck's routine during the rut in areas of high hunting pressure. During the night a few days before the first doe comes into estrus, a big trophy whitetail buck will spend his time chasing does around a food source. During the first light of morning, he will follow a group of does into a bedding area hoping one of them will come into estrus. He will harass them for awhile and then bed down with them. Sometimes he might post up in a spot that a lot of does travel by on their way back to a bedding area.

An hour or two after daylight the need to breed will take over and he will get up in search of more does. He then travels from one doe bedding area to another looking for a doe in estrus. He will use any good cover available in his travels. He will travel the downwind side of each bedding area trying to catch the sent of a hot doe. He then usually charges into the bedding area looking around as if he missed something. Then it is off to the next bedding area. When he does not find what he is looking for, and he gets tired of this game, he may bed down for awhile.

During the late afternoon he will post up in a spot between the bedding areas and a food source waiting for the does to travel by again. Then in the evening the whole process starts over until he finds that first doe in estrus.

The buck will then push his hot doe into some cover where they will not be bothered. He will spend a few days with her and breed her. When they are done he will usually wait until nightfall and will quickly find a new doe in estrus to service. After the last doe comes out of estrus this process continues for a few days until he is certain the rut is over. Then he will retire to thick cover to recover from the strains of rut.

As you can see from this scenario, this is why you should set up in funnels between the bedding areas and on the downwind side of those bedding areas. Do not miss out on this great opportunity as this could be your best chance of the year to take home the buck of a lifetime.

It is great to be in the woods in November.

Chapter 12

Late Season

Late season is usually considered late December through the end of January, if your hunting season extends until then. This should be considered the second best time of year to tag a trophy whitetail buck. This is due to the fact that the animals will give up safety to find food for survival during this harsh time of year. This is a great advantage to the late season hunter.

Herding

During this time of year your properties will either hold deer or nothing at all. Deer have a tendency to herd up in groups at this time of year. The bucks will herd up along with the does. The good news is that if your property does hold deer they are usually concentrated and there are many animals. The bad news is that there may not be one trophy buck among them.

In many areas, the best protected area for deer to herd up in is usually some type of park or camp. Also, it could be within the city limits or a large chunk of property that does not allow hunting. This could be good or bad depending on whether you have permission to hunt next to one of these sanctuaries.

A good late season buck.

Food Sources

The deer at this time of year will usually herd up in some undisturbed cover near a good food source. This food source is usually cut corn or soybeans before the fields are plowed under. Where there are no such food sources the deer's metabolism usually changes over to where they just live off grass and twigs of certain trees and plants.

Hunting Open Fields

Normally at this time of year cover is sparse for a hunter to hide in. Many times the woods are so crunchy under foot that it is hard to get close to where the deer bed without spooking them. This usually leaves you to hunt around the food source which is mainly open fields.

The trees at this time of year usually afford little cover for the hunter to hide in from the dozens of eyes. Also, the deer may have a tendency to move quickly out into the open field far from cover to use the open space as protection from predators.

Pit style blinds work well in this situation. If the deer can look over your blind, they seem to be much calmer. Furthermore this is where lying prone on the ground with a crossbow, where legal, is a good strategy. If snow is on the ground, snow camouflage works great. Other hunters wear grass style camouflage and sometimes lay behind a small log or a small pile of brush. You might have to use your imagination, but the payoff could be great.

Bait

The use of bait was covered in chapter nine. If it is legal in your state, it can help you control where the deer travel and feed. If you use this technique properly it can be one of your most productive strategies in the late season.

Cover can be sparse in the late season.

Bedding Close to Food

One problem for the hunter at this time of year is that the deer will bed as close to their food source as they can. This is to conserve energy. If they bed too far from your location or their food source, they will not get to you before legal shooting time expires. If they bed too close to their food source, you will not be able to get set up on them without alerting them to the fact you are there. There is one trick that may fool them though.

Many nice bucks are taken in the late season.

Two In One Out

One way to misdirect the deer herd to your presence is to walk into your stand with a friend. Do not worry about making noise as you want the deer to know you are there. After waiting until you are set, up your friend should leave making some noise as they go away. Deer do not count well and many times they will think you have left and come out shortly thinking all is safe. This should keep you thinking!

Chapter 13

Odds-n-Ends

This chapter is about a few things that just did not seem to fit anywhere else in this book. This is just the opinions of one writer, and you should always go with your heart.

Leasing

Leasing is a sore subject for many hunters. The terrible truth of the matter is that if you want to hunt trophy whitetail bucks sooner or later you will have to get involved in some sort of lease arrangement. In the future this may be the only way to control the hunting pressure on a piece of property.

Landowners and farmers are constantly looking for ways to increase their income today. To hunt on their property is a privilege and the landowners rightfully feel they should get some compensation for letting you trespass and hunt on their land. Furthermore, it gives the hunter a good feeling knowing exactly who and how the land is to be hunted.

If you do decide to enter a lease agreement with someone, make sure it is with a good group of people. Always make sure things are fair for all interested parties. Remember your goals as a trophy hunter, but do not forget that this sport is supposed to be enjoyable.

The real truth of the matter is that if you do not enter a lease agreement soon you may be on the outside looking in.

Sooner or later you will have to get a lease to hunt bucks like this.

Sportsmanship and Ethics

Sportsmanship and ethics should not be taken lightly. If you decide to chase trophy whitetails, you will forever be watched carefully by other hunters and the law. You must live and hunt with the highest standards. Never get involved in any unethical situation(s) or with any unethical hunter(s). To break a law in the pursuit of a trophy buck is completely wrong on all accounts.

Moreover, please respect the right of all other hunters and landowners even if they do not enjoy your sport the same way as you do. Never encroach on another hunter even if he is hunting in a different fashion than you. When asking for permission to hunt someone's property always ask if they have given permission to other hunters, and if they have, please decline even if you get permission. You would not want someone moving in on property you have hunted for years.

Keep in mind that unethical hunters make the news and do a terrible injustice to our sport and to responsible hunters.

Hunting Does

For years there has been much controversy about hunting does. The hunting community is finally realizing that managing the number of does is a form of good game management. In most highly hunted areas the doe-to-buck ratio is way out of whack in favor of the does. You should want your doe-to-buck ratio on your properties to be as close to one-to-one as possible.

The problem for today's trophy whitetail hunter in highly pressured areas is the fact that this is unrealistic. Today's hunting properties are so small that, if you eliminated every doe you saw, you would only move the animals onto the neighbor's property and destroy all trophy potential on your own. This is the one and only reason you should not harass or shoot does on your property. Hopefully the neighbors will thin the doe herd for you and make your property a sanctuary for them and a few mature bucks.

Choose wisely when and where to shoot does.

Immature Bucks

Only two facts apply to immature bucks. Number one, if you shoot them they will not have a chance to grow into a mature trophy bucks. Number two, it is a fact that the smallest yearling or spike buck can grow into a high scoring monster.

Gun Hunting

This book is geared towards bow hunting. The truth is that any strategy that works well with bow hunting will work great when gun hunting. Gun hunting is the one strategy where you can rely purely on forced movement of animals. What this means is, that if a big buck is considered completely nocturnal and refuses to come out from hiding during daylight hours, you can still step on him and make him move. During the correct season with a gun in your hands, you have the best chance of putting this type of animal on the ground.

Summer vs. Winter Coats

One final weird thought. Many people ask why does a deer's summer coat look red and its' winter coat look brown? One thought is that most predators other than man are color blind. To a color blind animal the closest hue to green is red. Since it would be hard for a deer to grow green hair in the summer maybe evolution has helped them hide from predators in the summer by giving them red coats. Then in the winter their brown coats blend in with the bleak brown surrounding of winter.

Gun hunting will extend your trophy hunting possibilities.

Chapter 14

Three Seasons

There I stood with a puzzled look on my face. It was the beginning of the deer hunting season, and I had made the decision this year to hunt mature trophy bucks only.

After taking close to seventy whitetails with a recurve bow, here I stood with one of those fancy compound bows with wheels. A terrible tree stand accident while setting stands in February a few years back seemed to make a compound bow a better option for my aching body. The truth was that every time a monster buck showed up in range I could never make it happen with my recurve. I guess I wanted it too bad to pull it off.

This season I had decided to branch out on my own. This was due to differences in opinion and goals with a former hunting partner. After working all spring, I had found some great new farms in a couple of different counties that showed promise for trophy bucks. The landowners I met this year will always be considered my friends, even though I do not hunt some of those same farms today.

Season One

It was the first week of October in Michigan and I was sitting one evening in a fencerow at the corner of a small woodlot between two standing cornfields. A good breeze was blowing from the southwest. It was very hot, and I was facing north waiting for a big buck to come out of the woodlot and head down the fencerow to the small ditch just south of me for a drink of water.

It was about an hour before dark. I looked over my shoulder and here he came. He was about a one hundred and forty inch eight point buck probably four and a half years old. He was coming from the south after leaving the standing corn and had probably already drunk from the ditch. This is where I learned my first lesson on where big bucks bed.

He was heading for the woodlot to probably feed on acorns. As he passed my tree I put what I thought was the perfect shot on him as he was quartering away. I had hit him in the last rib on the near side and the far shoulder on the opposite side. I was ecstatic!

I figured he would just jump into the small woodlot and die. After waiting until just after dark, I got down from my tree. I did not find blood at the site of the hit due to the fact the arrow had not come out the far side. I was still in pain from my recent accident and all alone so I decided to go home and bring back help in the morning. It would be plenty cold that night, and I did not figure he went too far.

After arriving with help at daylight the following morning, we began to track my animal. Somehow he had the energy to make it out the other side of the woodlot and across a cut cornfield. We tracked him to where he had fallen between two farmhouses about one hundred yards from the road. Here we found fresh tire tracks, a few tufts of hair, and some blood at the end of the trail. I was in shock. Someone had stolen my first trophy buck!!

I went to all of the farmhouses in the area trying to find out any information on my buck. No one seemed to know anything. I would find out years later that one of the houses I had visited did in fact have my deer. Little did I know that my future hunting partner had skinned the big eight point out for these people the following day without knowing this was my buck.

I spent the rest of the fall season trying to connect with one of the other big bucks I knew was in the area. Later that fall I did have a couple of other encounters with big bucks, but could not make it happen. I was using calls, rattling horns and decoys without much success. I called in a lot of small bucks, but I found the mature bucks did not tolerate these tactics, and soon they became nocturnal or avoided my farms all together. Other problems I was experiencing were the many trespassers on my farms and the heavy hunting pressure on the adjoining and surrounding farms.

The Michigan season finally came to a close at the end of December and all I had left to hunt was Ohio. It was January 11th and I was sitting this evening on a small piece of property hoping something would happen. Then about an hour before dark a large buck came over the hill pushing four does. At fifteen yards I took him with a perfect shot that went through both lungs. He made it only thirty yards and fell in the snow. When I reached him I found out that he was a very large mature seven pointer with a deformed left horn. He would later weigh in at two hundred and five pounds dressed out.

I had my cell phone on me and refused to leave my prize this time as I called for help to drag him out. I was finally the proud owner of my first trophy buck.

My first trophy buck.

Season Two

I was pumped for my second season of trophy hunting. I was just starting to get to know my present hunting partner, Mark. Little did I know at the time that he would become my mentor and the great friend and hunting partner that he is today.

The first week of October caught me sitting one evening in a thicket next to a prime food source. This was Ohio and fifty yards away was a great sanctuary. Two hours before dark a large buck approached. I double lunged him at ten yards. He only took a few steps and expired.

I climbed down from my stand and approached my trophy. This was the first time I had an experience with ground shrinkage. The buck that I thought was a large eight point now lay before me as a big six. Thankfully he was still a great buck, and I was very happy to have my second trophy buck. Unfortunately, we get only one buck tag for Ohio, and mine was now filled.

I continued hunting Michigan for the rest of the season. It was now November 14th, the day before gun season. The pressure from other hunters in the woods this season had been tremendous. I had not seen any shooters within range as many small bucks passed by me in a couple of funnels. What I had noticed were a few big bucks that had bedded in some sparse fencerows as they hid from all the hunters in the woods. The problem was that I was unable to slip up on them with my bow.

As I sat there that morning, I started to slip back to my old ways. I told myself if any buck came within range that had eight points or more that I would take him. Twenty minutes later I looked over and a young eight pointer was approaching. The next thing I knew he had an arrow shot through him. He went about one hundred yards before giving up the ghost.

As I walked up to him, I could not believe what I had just done. This was not the kind of animal I was hunting for. He had all the character to grow into an impressive animal, but he wasn't quite there yet! He is now mounted

The buck I thought was a large eight point now lay before me as a big six.

and hanging on my wall. He is a reminder of my mistakes and what not to do.

Michigan allows a hunter to take two bucks in one season. For this reason I decided to get it back together. I hung a stand out in one of the fencerows that I had seen those big bucks in for next day's gun season.

As the sun broke over the horizon the next day, I had already heard at least a dozen shots from my stand. About fifteen minutes later I noticed three does and two bucks slip into a fencerow across the road about three quarters of a mile away. Through my binoculars I could tell one of the bucks was a nice eight point. The other buck though was a mature buck carrying a wall of tines on his head. I was excited because I had permission to hunt that section of land.

I shot the massive eleven pointer at thirty yards.

It had been cold and frosty the night before, and the ground and leaves were noisy to walk on. I decided to wait until the sun had melted the frost before I made an attempt to stalk these deer. About forty-five minutes later I made my move.

I slipped out of my stand and worked my way across the road. The deer were about a half mile out at the end of the fencerow. The wind was good and about twenty minutes later, as I paralleled the fencerow; I was approaching the last forty yards without seeing neither hide nor hair of a deer yet.

I stood there wondering what my next move was when the large buck pushed the eight pointer out from the fencerow. I shot the massive eleven pointer at thirty yards. When he fell, I became the proud hunter who tagged the ninth largest buck taken in Michigan that season.

Season Three

After such a great second season this season started out to be quite a mess. I barely had time to hunt during the month of October. For that reason I made up for lost time in November by taking more time away from work to hunt.

Mid-afternoon on the first of November found me relocating a stand. This was due to the changing density of cover after leaf drop and the changing mood of the deer in preparation for the rut.

I had just set a stand in my tree of choice when I heard branches breaking on the other side of the gully. Out of the far hawthorn thicket and up my side of the gully came three bucks. One was a year and a half old eight point, and the second was a one hundred forty inch class animal. The third animal was one of the largest whitetails I had ever seen. He stopped ten yards from my stand. There I stood trying to hide in my tree in blue jeans and a red flannel shirt.

It was a good thing that I had worn my rubber boots and sprayed down with scent shield, as he never knew I was there. While I tried to judge the size of his rack he slowly slipped down the gully and disappeared. About fifteen minutes later the other two bucks followed. I do not know if I would have been able to take a shot, but I had broken my golden rule of never going into the woods during hunting season without my bow.

The rest of November did not get much better. November eleventh was the morning of the full moon, also known as the rutting moon. I saw deer movement all morning. At 7:30 in the morning, a year and a half old buck with half his rack broken off approached my stand. At 8:30 I passed on a two and a half year old eight pointer. I took a picture of him at six yards instead.

Then at 9:30 in the morning a large mature eight point came in. I then proceeded to screw up my first chance at a mature buck this year by shooting low at less than twenty yards.

November fourteenth was the day before Michigan's gun season. I hunted most of the day with my bow and passed on a five point, a seven point and an eight point at twelve yards or less. I did see a mature eight point early in the afternoon, but did not get a shot.

November fifteenth was the opening day of Michigan's gun season. This was the day of unethical hunters. At 8:30 in the morning I had located a huge buck and had closed the distance to him to about two hundred yards while he tended a doe. I hunt in the shotgun-only section of Michigan so attempting a shot was out of the question at this point.

While contemplating my next move a pickup truck came down the county road and stopped. The hunter proceeded to take shots at the buck from the back of his truck. He wounded him at about two hundred yards and later lost him.

Upset I went back to Ohio for an evening bow hunt only to find my stand stolen. This forced me to relocate to another stand farther down the ravine I was hunting. From this stand I sat and watched as the monster buck I had seen earlier in November walked under the tree where the stolen stand had been. My season seemed to be unraveling on me.

The afternoon of November 18th found me once again hunting the same area. Two does came through at 3:30 in the afternoon followed approximately one hour later by my monster buck. I drew on him twice, once at twenty-eight yards and once at twenty-five yards. Unfortunately, he did not give me a shot as he walked away.

I took a picture of this buck at six yards.

I have always wanted to harvest a mature buck on Thanksgiving Day. On the morning of Thanksgiving I was in my stand well before first light. At 9:30 in the morning a twenty-inch wide three and a half year old animal came in to my set up. He had a few broken tines, so I passed on him. I later wondered if I had made a mistake.

November finally ended, My diary indicated that I had went on twenty two hunts on which I had seen one hundred and eight whitetails of which I passed on sixty-two at less than twenty yards. During this same time, I had seen twenty-two bucks, fifteen of which I had passed on. Eight of those bucks were bucks that scored between one hundred twenty and one hundred seventy plus inches. I thought to myself how could I have not connected yet.

The first week of December was the Ohio gun season, and I did not get a chance to hunt. On December 9th I decided to go on an evening bow hunt due to a few factors.

Old Bullseye

First, it was a couple of days after the full moon, and I was expecting that any does that were not bred last month would be about ready to go into estrus again. This with colder temperatures and fresh snow should have deer on the move. At 4:45 in the evening I noticed six or eight does milling around in the hawthorns about sixty yards away. Then I looked up as a deer approached my stand. I could not believe it but my monster buck was the first animal to walk by. He offered me a broadside shot at fifteen yards finalizing my second dream season in a row.

    I decided to call this buck Bullseye because he had a second throat patch that looks like a perfect bull's eye. He is a mainframe eight point with over a twenty-four inch inside spread and has a gross score of over one hundred and seventy seven inches. I guess the third season was a charm. From that season on I have dedicated myself to hunting trophy whitetails year-round.

***Practice true sportsmanship and good luck shall be your reward.**

Cabin Fever Publications

Quick Order Form

To order more copies of Year-Round Trophy Whitetails

Internet orders: Trophy-Whitetails.com

Telephone orders: 419-885-2535
Have your credit card ready.

Fax orders: 419-885-1260

Postal orders: Cabin Fever Publications
PO Box 366
Sylvania, Ohio 43560

Please send book(s) to:

Name: _____

Address: _____

City: _____ State: _____ Zip: _____

Price: $24.95 each.

Shipping and handling: $4.00 for first book. $2.00 for each additional book. Canadian S&H: $6.00/book.

Payment:

Check/Money Order ___   Mastercard ___   Visa ___

Card #: _____

Name on card: _____

Expiration date: _____

Ohio residents please add 6.75% sales tax.

See us at www.trophy-whitetails.com